MIGHTY MEN NEEDED

A TIMELESS REVELATION ON CHURCH LEADERSHIP

MIGHTY
MEN
NEEDED

Timely Instructions for Today's Leaders and a
Necessary Equipping for Tomorrow's Frontrunners

Temidayo Adewole

XULON PRESS

Xulon Press
2301 Lucien Way #415
Maitland, FL 32751
407.339.4217
www.xulonpress.com

For inquiries and bulk distribution, please contact:
The Oracles of God
P.O. Box 25075,
Truro, NS
Canada
B2N 7B8
Email: oracles@rehobothsprings.ca

Unless otherwise indicated, Scripture quotations taken from the King
James Version (KJV) – *public domain.*

Paperback ISBN-13: 978-1-6628-0160-0
Library of Congress Control Number: 2020921839
Ebook ISBN-13: 978-1-6628-0161-7

DEDICATION

This book is dedicated to:
God the Father who gave His only begotten Son,
Jesus Christ our Lord and Savior who gave His life a propitiation for our sins,
The Holy Spirit who continues to beckon on all men to come to the knowledge of truth.

TABLE OF CONTENTS

ACKNOWLEDGMENT

I thank Deborah, my wife and burden-bearer, who has tirelessly, selflessly, and lovingly labored with me for the Lord in many places, and under several difficult circumstances. May the Lord reward the hours of sleep and comfort you invested and sacrificed while editing this book.

And to Daniel and 'Dara, thank you for your understanding and prayers all through the way.

THIS BOOK AND YOU

Several churches are in trouble today because leadership decisions are being exalted above the Word of God. In many assemblies, countless people saddled with great responsibilities were not given the necessary spiritual preparations.

Also, many church leaders are unknowingly destroying or limiting the persons that God had sent to them to fulfill His purpose in their ministry.

While stressing what today's leaders need to know, the book in your hand highlights all that tomorrow's leaders must do to be great. There is no doubt; it clarifies why many churches have remained stagnant in many places.

Mighty Men Needed is both a spiritual leaders' manual and a scriptural atlas for the laities. It is an asset for anyone that is destined to be great in God's service. After reading and applying the truths encountered in this book, I am sure you will lose interest in many failures celebrated as successes in numerous churches today.

It would take courage to read through this book as it unravels many unspoken truths and questions many traditions and theological views held "sacred" in the church, even though they oppose God's Word and His moral standards. As you read, you may stop at whatever point you feel the conviction and need to pray, before you continue.

Here is a book that will change your life, family, and ministry. It will help you walk circumspectly and to please God.

Temidayo Adewole

November 2020

ONE

ADULLAM

A Necessary Step to Greatness

*And three of the thirty chief went down, and came to David in the harvest time **unto the cave of Adullam:** and the troop of the Philistines pitched in the valley of Rephaim*
(2 Sam. 23:13)

The cave of Adullam is a significant locale in the life of David and his mighty men. For several years, it was both their spiritual base and retreat hideout. The story of David's rise and ascent to the throne would be incomplete without a necessary reference to the Cave of Adullam. What is the significance of this cave, and how applicable is this to believers today?

Incidentally, Adullam was that place where God molded the destinies of David's men. The transformation of many lives happened at Adullam. From this cave, David and his men discovered their purposes and pursued it. Could you think of any place like the cave of Adullam today? Can you consider your church a place where people can find God and His purpose for their lives? Do people who enter your church as distressed, discouraged, dissatisfied, disillusioned, delusional, depressed, disabled, and in debt still find refuge at the cross? In Adullam cave, David and his men would not make any decision about the battles of their lives until they have heard from God. We need to take a critical look at the situation of David and his men at this cave and learn some lessons that could help our lives and churches fulfill heaven's goal.

The description and exact location

David therefore departed thence, and **escaped to the cave Adullam**: *and when his brethren and all his father's house heard it, they went down thither to him* (1 Sam. 22:1).

The cave was so-called because it was near the city of Adullam. It was situated about twelve miles from the town of Bethlehem. It must have been so large as to house David and about six hundred men who came to meet him in the cave when he fled from Saul. "And David arose, **and he passed over with the six hundred men who were with him** unto Achish, the son of Maoch, king of Gath" (1 Sam. 27:2).

The description of this cave depicts a place where a man could explore as much as possible. Undoubtedly, it would have taken a great deal of adventure to search such a large room in the middle of nowhere. It is nonetheless instructive to see the good that came out of all the troubles David went through. If Saul had not been after David, he might not have sought out the cave, a place that later became the training ground from where the most formidable army of his day would rise. What are you going through presently? You can look around and seek the face of God, asking Him to open your eyes to the particular good that can proceed from your current, seemingly unfortunate situation.

The significance of Adullam

*Yet will I bring an heir unto thee, O inhabitant of Mareshah: he shall come unto **Adullam the glory of Israel*** (Mic. 1:15).

Cave means "fortress," while Adullam means "justice." Hence the cave of Adullam can be rightly interpreted as "the fortress of justice." What a beautiful discovery to note. Every believer needs a combination of both. Indeed, God used this cave to fortify and defend David. No wonder he wrote: *I will say of the Lord, He is my refuge and my fortress: my God; in him will I trust* (Ps. 91:10).

The cave of Adullam is symbolic of what God is to the believer. The glory of man depends largely on who is his fortress and justifier. No matter what the enemy may be doing against a child of God, if he or she continually resorts to God as a fortress, the story will always end on a note of victory. Who is your fortress? Are you sure God is your fortress? Who is your first point of call when you are faced with challenges? If God is not your fortress, you can be sure that disappointment is near. Affluence, occult powers, people, oratory power, relations, and influence will fail you. Anything less than God will not suffice. If you have made God your fortress, stay on course. You will surely see the beauty resident in trusting the Lord. As you continue to tarry with God, He will surely come and save you. "And ye shall seek me, and find me, when ye shall search for me with all your heart" (Jer. 29:11). God is committed to those who make Him their fortress.

It was a place of training and development

And every one that was in distress, and every one that was in debt, and every one that was discontented, gathered themselves unto him; and he became a captain over them: and there were with him about four hundred men (1 Sam. 22:2).

David did not only use the cave as a hideout from troubles. He also used it as a training base. The cave became a common ground to address all the problems in the lives of those surrounding him. Some were in debt, some in distress, and others were discounted in life. By application, the cave was where God turned the lives of all these men around to become the most potent force in the entire nation of Israel. Rather than stay in the cave and cry or murmur, David developed the men of low degree that were with him. Are you at a low point in your finances, career, or spiritual life? Look around and do something positive with whatever your hands find to do. It is quite surprising that a shepherd boy would stir up the leadership potentials within himself and develop an army from scratch.

This situation bolsters the fact that there are no dead churches, rather incapable leaders. The problems in families, nations, and churches rise and fall on leadership. Give a cold church to a fiery leader, and you will return after six months to find a vibrant church. The opposite is well evident in many denominations today.

The Wright brothers built the first aircraft in their bicycle shop. That was their cave of Adullam. Wherever you are today can become your cave of Adullam. A room in your house, your present position at work, your church, or your family can be your cave of Adullam. Stop dreaming about the palace; instead work with the cave of Adullam at hand. Life's success is a function of what you do with what destiny has placed in your hands. Your faithfulness in the cave guarantees your journey to the castle and secures your ascension to the throne.

It takes commitment and frequent visits

*David therefore departed thence, and **escaped to the cave Adullam**: and when his brethren and all his father's house heard it, they went down thither to him* (1 Sam. 22:1).

*And three of the thirty chief went down, and came to David in the harvest time **unto the cave of Adullam:** and the troop of the Philistines pitched in the valley of Rephaim* (2 Sam. 23:13).

For David, he found the cave of Adullam, and he often returned there for security and strategy. The cave became the site of their conventions, conferences, and strategy congresses. They wrapped their minds around their challenges, unraveled thoughts, and dispelled doubts and fears. By the time they went out, no man could stand before them. Even though it would take about four hours to walk from Bethlehem to the cave of Adullam, they made a commitment to be there. Such determination is a reprimand to Christians who would forbid the gathering of genuine believers on the grounds of flimsy excuses. Rather than rot away in the comfort of the city, they would rather pay the price and trek the distance to the place where their lives could become better.

Every believer needs to search for such places, fellowships, churches, or groups where they can freely pray and express their real spiritual state to God. No price is too high to pay to get to a place where you can get the best from God. You need a place where true Christianity is not just preached but practiced. No price is too much to get in touch with a mentor whose utterance would make a difference in your life. You must not settle for less when God still has more for you. You must always go for the best. You must reach until there is nothing left unreached and press forward until you have gone all the way with God. As you press on with God, the time will surely come when nations will search for you. You will be grateful that you have lived well.

REFLECTIONS ON CHAPTER ONE

The following questions may be used for personal reflections or group discussions:

1. Can you list some challenges that you are currently facing in your life or ministry?

i. _____

ii. _____

iii. _____

iv. _____

2. Can you think about how these challenges could make you stronger?

i. _____

ii. _____

iii. _____

iv. _____

3. Can you think of a person you could share those challenges with?

i. _____

4. During difficult times, could you think of a place, fellowship, or church that could be an Adullam for you?

i. _____

5. Have you found a mentor, place, fellowship, church, or group where your gifts and potentials can be stirred up to God's glory?

i. _____

ii. _____

6. Can you identify some folks you could mentor in your Adullam?

i. _____

ii. _____

iii. _____

iv. _____

7. In what other ways can you apply lessons learned in this chapter?

i. _____

ii. _____

iii. _____

TWO

THE THREE

Round Pegs in Round Holes

And the three mighty men brake through the host of the Philistines, and drew water out of the well of Bethlehem, that was by the gate, and took it, and brought it to David: *nevertheless he would not drink thereof, but poured it out unto the LORD. And he said, be it far from me, O LORD, that I should do this: is not this the blood of the men who went in jeopardy of their lives? therefore he would not drink it.* **These things did these three mighty men.**
(2 Sam. 23:16, 17)

It is notable in scripture that Christians ought to set their gaze upon the author and finisher of their faith. Yet, we cannot deny that "all scripture is given by inspiration of God, and is profitable for doctrine, for reproof, for correction, for instruction in righteousness: that the man of God may be perfect, thoroughly furnished unto all good works" (2 Tim. 3:16, 17).

Therefore, imitating these mighty men, who were exceptionally recognized in scriptures, focusing intently upon their lives to glean divine instructions of eternal relevance, becomes a necessity for those who desire to stand out in ministry, career, and in every other sphere of life. This troika shall be our focus before we delve into the lives of the rest of the mighty men.

Who are these triumvirate warriors?

1. Adino, the Eznite;

2. Eleazar, the son of Dodo the Ahohite; and

3. Shamma, the son of Agee the Hararite.

These three men came to the rescue of David, the anointed of the Lord, while he was hiding inside the cave of Adullam at a very dangerous time because the enemy's troops had pitched their tents in the valley of Rephaim to intercept the people's harvest. A careful reflection on how they attained this height is of utmost importance. By the etymology of their names, some of these men were non-Israelites, yet they attained the highest seat in a foreign land! This is quite an admonitory challenge to people who give excuses for their inability to excel in foreign lands. Joseph, Daniel, Esther, Mordecai, and many others were refugees and immigrants at certain times of their lives, yet they all became noble and did not stand before mean men. You may be in a foreign country yet succeed very well if you do something with what you are reading and learning from this book.

Gleanings from their lives and exploits

1. Adino the Eznite
the same was Adino the Eznite (2 Sam. 23:8).

As established in the scriptures, his real name was not Adino, rather Jashobeam! Adino means **"his ornament,"** for indeed, he was an ornament to David. He added color to David's inherent skills, dexterity, and ingenuity on the battlefield. In every sphere of life, no successful leader would deny being surrounded or supported by some committed workers and laborers of like passion who devote themselves faithfully and steadfastly to his purpose and vision. The successes of Moses, Paul the apostle, and our Lord Jesus Christ attested to this fact, and that is the story of many organizations and churches in contemporary times.

To have the devotion of such a man is an adornment. Such men would always meet the desire of any leader of David's stature and rank. David's victory in every battle and over the sons of Belial are testimonials that he was surrounded by men described by this man's name. This also agrees with what David meant when he said, "but the man who shall touch them (sons of Belial) must be fenced with iron and the staff of a spear" (2 Sam. 23: 7). All the other names by which Jashobeam was called were only encomiums to describe him as a warrior!

With whom are you surrounding yourself, and for what purposes are they around you? Are they truly making your life more beautiful to behold? Are you a leader surrounded by traitors and difficult people? You can stand upon the revelation of this word to make your request known to God. Ask God to send men who are Adinos and Eznites into your team and ministry, men who would do anything to quench your thirst. You need men who would labor tirelessly, as unto God. However, when such men come to labor for God under your leadership, they must not be abused. Leaders must never take the labor of men who put their lives in their hands for granted. Their efforts must be considered a sacrifice to God and not for the glory or ego or any man. They must be appreciated and acknowledged; otherwise, they might be lost to the disadvantage of God's kingdom.

He was the Tachmonite

The Tachmonite that sat in the seat, chief among the captains; the same was Adino the Eznite (2 Sam. 23:8).

Tachmonite means, **"Thou will make me wise."** The use of the article *'the'* is noteworthy as he was the only Tachmonite mentioned in God's Book. We did not hear of any other Tachmonite. However, he did not jump down from the sky. He was born, he had brethren, and he had a nationality. Going by the "common wishes," all Tachmonites are supposedly called to be wise. Why was Adino the only one who went beyond and above insignificance, mediocrity, and oblivion?

Friend, your name may be "Grace," but that does not mean that you will automatically have the grace to live above sin. It is not all "Joys" who are glad, and not all who are named "Faith" are in the faith. It then presupposes that being called by a Christian name is not enough. Being decorated with the title of a pastor, evangelist, prophet, teacher, or an apostle does not translate into the acquiring of the necessary spiritual gifts required to function profitably and effectively in those spiritual offices. There are gifts needed for each of the offices. Essentially, you may be called a Tachmonite, but that would not automatically translate into wisdom within you. Pastoral ordination does not necessarily result in the ministerial success and fulfillment. Laying on of hands is not enough; the gift must be coveted and stirred. Deliberate works of faith and a life devoted to study, prayers, and fasting are all necessary before God would be pleased to glorify Himself in any mortal man. *Study to shew thyself approved unto God, a workman who needeth not to be ashamed, rightly dividing the word of truth* (2 Tim. 2:15).

Jesus called the apostles and commissioned them, yet he sternly warned them not to venture "going" until the promised enduement from the Father is released upon them! If those men and women who ate, dined, walked, and worked with the Son of God while he was here on earth had to wait for ten full days before the heavens would open unto them, how is it we do not sense the beckoning of the Lord to us today? Why does it sound strange when you hear God telling you to wait in the place where He makes His men before launching out today? Could this not be the reason for the many years in ministry without having any tangible harvest to show for it? Is it not wiser to wait upon God until His Holy Spirit breathes upon every word that proceeds from your mouth afterward? Is it not more profitable to fast and pray ten days, then go out and preach a sermon that will bring 3,000 souls unto Christ?

Probably, this situation describes what you are going through in your ministry. Set out time to wait upon God. Determine to seek His face until your heaven is flung open by the heavenly Father.

For this man to have joined himself unto David confirms that Adino lived up to his name. Using some mathematical expression to convey an allusion about the various categories of men you might come across in life, you can categorize the people in or around your life into four groups, namely: adders, subtracters, dividers, and multipliers. The **adders** are those who add value to your life. The **subtracters** only receive and give you nothing while the **dividers** are everywhere, occupying the seats of Delilah and Joseph's brothers. The job description of the dividers is to kill, steal, and destroy. Last, we have the **multipliers**—these are those who replicate themselves in others! In every organization, family, church, and society, multipliers are always the fewest.

Thus, this Tachmonite was very wise to have looked for someone who could make him fulfill the purpose of his name—"to be made wise." He understood ahead of time that "wisdom is the principal thing" (Prov. 4:7). It is therefore not a surprise that he attained the highest seat in his chosen career. He became one of the most significant voices in the most powerful military of his generation. "He that walketh with wise men shall be wise: but a companion of fools shall be destroyed"

(Prov. 13:20). Who are your friends? Are they investing wisdom in you? If one iron does not sharpen another iron, something is fundamentally wrong. *Iron sharpeneth iron; so a man sharpeneth the countenance of his friend* (Prov. 27:17).

Your countenance is a typical reflection of your inward disposition. It epitomizes the expression of your face, and it could tell much about your spiritual, financial, emotional, and professional wellbeing. Your countenance is you! Hence, if those you associate with do not improve your outlook toward God and His purpose for your life, it may be the right time for you to begin to redefine your relationship with them. Be wise like the only Tachmonite who made it into God's book. Seek mentorship, fellowship, connection, and friendship that would help multiply the talents and gifts of God in your life. You have only one life. Manage it well. There is no spare.

He was the one that sat at the seat

*"The Tachmonite **that sat in the seat**, chief among the captains; the same was Adino the Eznite"* (2 Sam. 23:8). Who else should sit at the seat if not a man who has become an Adino? For your team to succeed, you must put the round pegs into round holes. Evangelist Reinhard Bonnke was that blessed man who, after leading an astounding 60 million people to Christ at the age of seventy, passed the baton of his ministry, Christ for All Nations, to twenty-nine-year-old Evangelist Daniel Kolenda saying, **"the anointed must be appointed."**

Who is sitting on "the seat" of leadership and decision-making in your church or ministry? While maturity is essential, the appointment into the leadership position in the church must not be preconditioned only on age. Even in the Old Testament, the ability of a leader is a prioritized requirement in the sight of God. While there are several other requirements highlighted by God, the need for capacity always appears on top of the list.

> *Moreover thou shalt provide out of all the people* ***able men***, *such as fear God, men of truth, hating covetousness; and place such over them, to be rulers of thousands, and rulers of hundreds, rulers of fifties, and rulers of tens* (Exod. 18:21).

> *And Moses chose* ***able men*** *out of all Israel, and made them heads over the people, rulers of thousands, rulers of hundreds, rulers of fifties, and rulers of tens* (Exod. 18:25).

In the New Testament, the Holy Spirit is the significant ability-base of God's servants. He empowers and equips the believer for effective service. It always results in God's glory when you appoint men following God's prescribed pattern. The results of such decisions are evident in Scriptures and several ministries worldwide.

... and they chose Stephen, ***a man full of faith and of the Holy Ghost*** (Acts 6:5).

And Stephen, ***full of faith and power, did great wonders and miracles*** *among the people* (Acts 6:8).

It was evident in Scriptures that any man who is chosen based on how many years they have been in the church, family ties, or quota system does not always run well with the vision of the Lord. Before the Holy Spirit's Baptism came upon the disciples of Jesus, they used the Old Testament method of casting of lots to appoint. We never heard of anything tangible about the ministry of that man they appointed by such a process. Jesus told the disciples to wait. He did not ask them to ordain a replacement for Judas. Many churches are still making this crucial mistake today. They appoint and ordain people just because they have been to Bible school or because they have influence or affluence when the Lord has not told them to do so. Of course, this is an indication that the Lord is not leading such leaders. Before Jesus appointed the twelve, He spent time praying. No wonder he selected the faithful eleven and one betrayal, who would perfect the essence of His coming. On the contrary, the apostles already appointed two men before they sought the face of God for who should be a replacement for Judas. Let us look at what they did – they already appointed two people before they prayed and cast lots!

*And **they appointed two**, Joseph called Barsabas, who was surnamed Justus, and Matthias. And **they prayed,** and said, thou, Lord, which knowest the hearts of all men, **shew whether of these two thou hast chosen**, that he may take part of this ministry and apostleship, from which Judas by transgression fell, that he might go to his own place. And **they gave forth their lots**; and the lot fell upon Matthias; and he was numbered with the eleven apostles* (Acts 1:23-26).

What if God's choice was neither of these two men they brought before God? This kind of appointment was only an arrangement of men and not by the Holy Ghost. Their reason for Joseph and Matthias was based on how many years these two men had been with them (Acts 1:21). This is what happens when leadership is void of divine access to the heart of God.

The divine replacement for Judas was Paul the apostle, not Matthias. Paul confirmed it, and this was obvious in the record of scriptures.

Paul, an apostle, (not of men, neither by man, but by Jesus Christ, and God the Father, who raised him from the dead) – Gal. 1:1.

Paul deliberately put an emphasis on the scriptural verse above to let the church know that there is a difference between a man-appointed apostle and a God-appointed one. The difference is clear.

A true leader must not yield to the temptation of using people, based on how long they have been in the church. Even if there are no able men around, the requisite is to pray to the God of the harvest. Those appointed must be the folks who would do the service, not just the founding members of the church.

In many churches, those who occupy leadership seats have not had a personal encounter with the Lord of the work. Little wonder the seat is always too hot for them. Preaching in many places is nothing more than a history class. For the most part, Christianity has become theoretical rather than practical. Does it not bother you that there is no one to pray for the sick? Those who are possessed are being counseled, rather than being delivered! Congregants are quiet but worried! Everyone seems to be asking—*If the Lord be with us, why then is all this befallen us? And where be all his miracles which our fathers told us of...?"* (Judg. 6:13a). *"Why is it that we see not our signs? Why is there is no more any prophet? Why is there none among us any that knoweth how long? (Ps. 74:9). The harvest is past, the summer is ended, and we are not saved ... is there no balm in Gilead; is there no physician there? why then is not the health of the daughter of my people recovered?* (Jer. 18:22).

How is it that people had become church overseers when God never called them into the ministry? If a man is never called, how can he run well? There can be no revival until those who are called and anointed are appointed to the principal seats of ministry. Such churches and movements will be no better than lecture theaters where doctrines are turned over week in and week out without anything to show for it in the lives of the members other than the perfection of hypocrisy, strife, competition, and regular confession of sins.

He was chief among captains

*The Tachmonite that sat in the seat, **chief among the captains**; the same was Adino the Eznite* (2 Sam. 23:8).

Becoming a captain in David's army was an enormous task, and it was an even more super-duty to become chief among the captains. To be chief implies that he was a thinktank. He was someone who brought tangible ideas to the table at all times. He always had something to offer as a leader. He was not a figurehead. It also implies that he had to be at the forefront when danger was near. These and many more were the duties saddled upon the shoulder of he who would be chief. The office was neither a flower title nor a political decoration.

In those days, to be the chief went beyond the uniform design; it was a matter of how much a man was capable of doing when duty called or danger neared. Here comes the question again, who are the chiefs in your church or ministry? On what basis were they appointed? Did not even our Lord and Savior Jesus Christ raise the bar of leadership in Matthew 20:27 when He said, "Whosoever will be chief among you, let him be your servant"?

Some pastors declare fasting for their members while they feast away in their offices and homes. Some others announce evangelism, but they neither show up nor participate. The account presented by the lives of these men is a clarion call to review how you select and appoint men and women into the service of the Lord. No wonder the army of David never lost any battle. May you not fail in your leadership assignment.

He was someone who could kill 300 at a time

*He lifted up his spear against **three hundred** slain by him at one time* (1 Chron. 11:11).

In David's army, might and strength are necessary criteria that wins the chiefest seat for any man. Since both Abishai, the brother of Joab, and Adino killed three hundred; they should be of equal ranking. However, Adino later went ahead of this feat. Therefore, it is logical to believe that the narrative where Adino was said to have slain three hundred at one time was before the storyline, submitted toward the close of David's life, where he was said to have killed eight hundred at another time. He went above and beyond the level of Abishai. He pressed further unto greater heights.

He went beyond his contemporaries, to kill 800 at a time

The Tachmonite that sat in the seat, chief among the captains; **the same was Adino the Eznite:** *he lift up his spear against* **eight hundred,** *whom he slew at one time* (2 Sam. 23:8b).

David's figurative expression about a man being fenced by iron and the staff of a spear might be about these men who surrounded him into exploits and victories. Such interpretation posits each of these mighty men who surrounded David as men with the cutting efficiency of a spear and impenetrability of iron. It is quite interesting and more convincing to discover that the root meaning of Eznite means sharp, strong, and spear! Eznite was not just an adjectival reference for a nation. Instead, it was a character reference to the strength of a man who had developed himself to attain a higher degree than his equals. As a minister, it is possible to find some of your contemporaries doing better than you in ministry. Do not succumb to the spirit of criticism and derogation toward those who are doing better than you. Why not covet the gift and pay the price?

Then Peter opened his mouth, and said, **of a truth I perceive that God is no respecter of persons: but in every nation he that feareth him, and worketh righteousness, is accepted**

with him (Acts 10:34, 35). Indeed, God is not a respecter of persons. If you do what they did, you will get what they got. Those who have been in the church for long and have long stopped growing and developing may not like to see young men become great. They would do everything within and beyond their capacity to frustrate younger men and women from rising above them. Unfortunately, if such do not repent, they usually won't end well.

Here is a mortal man who grew in physical strength and military prowess until he became a sharp threshing instrument—An Eznite—**sharp** man, **strong** man, and **spear** of a man! Friend, how is it going with you? Do you have a holy desire to taste what it means to be an Eznite before you exit this world? How is your spiritual strength? Are you getting stronger or growing older but weaker in prayer and character?

2. Eleazar, the son of Dodo the Ahohite

And after him was Eleazar the son of Dodo the Ahohite, one of the three mighty men with David, when they defied the Philistines that were there gathered together to battle, and the men of Israel were gone away: he arose, and smote the Philistines until his hand was weary, and his hand clave unto the sword: and the Lord wrought a great victory that day; and the people returned after him only to spoil (2 Sam. 23:9,10).

He also became one of the three mighty men with David

...Eleazar the son of Dodo the Ahohite, one of the three mighty men with David (2 Sam. 23:9).

There are different categories of men in David's army. Eleazar chose to be among the three mighty. What are your goals in life, ministry, or career? Do you desire to make an impact with your

God-given talents and gifts? Do you see yourself rising to the level of the top three on the list of achievers in your field or ministry? During my high school days, we were taught a song culled from the words of a poem composed by Tai Solarin. Tai was the founding principal of Mayflower Secondary School, Nigeria. Even though He was a renowned atheist, he succeeded in reproducing the ethical aspects of his life in the character of almost all his students who had consequently gone everywhere in the world to make significant impacts and achievements in life.

You can become whatever you choose to be.
No king, no lord, no knave can say us nay
For we believe that man is a potential doctor,
Lawyer or cook or dwarf or giant whichever,
He sets his mind to be; we shall be giants;
And therefore, we shall work and work and work and work,
Even if we must work, work our fingers to the bone, so may it be.

He instilled in his students the principle of diligence and hard work. Honestly, "as a man *thinketh in his heart, so is he*" (Prov. 23:7). It is not possible to be diligent in every way and end up standing before mean men. Stop complaining about how miserable your situation is or how badly your boss or church is doing things. Begin to do something with your time, talent, and treasures.

Eleazar in this passage refused to end among the ranks and files of ordinary men of his generation. He chose to work toward greatness, and he became great.

He stood with the king when others were away

When they defied the Philistines that were there gathered together to battle, and the men of Israel were gone away: he arose, and smote the Philistines until his hand was weary, and his hand clave unto the sword: and the Lord wrought a great victory that day; and the people returned after him only to spoil (2 Sam. 23:9, 10).

Every leader surely needs the support of someone in one way or another. A single tree can never make a forest. Here is an essential secret of David's success. He surrounded himself with men of like passion. During this time, there was an invasion of Israel. David and his army had to defy the Philistines who were gathered together there to battle against them. At that particular time, the men of Israel were not around. Only Eleazar was with David, and it was a memory that lives on, even after both men were gone. The person who is with you at such a time when life gets dreary and weary will inevitably determine how you will come out of such situations.

Who is standing with you in what you are going through? Every person living with a purpose and a dream always goes through one challenge or the other. The reason for this is evident in Scripture. Every open door attracts several adversaries sent by the archenemy, Satan, who is always bothered about every man anointed of the Lord. That is why those who are under, around, or over them must be extremely careful as Satan may unwittingly use even them to frustrate God's purpose in their lives. This is what happened in the case of David and Christ. *"The kings of the earth set themselves, and the rulers take counsel together, **against the Lord, and against his anointed"*** (Ps. 2:2).

He was the man who arose

He arose, and smote the Philistines until his hand was weary, and his hand clave unto the sword: and the Lord wrought a great victory that day; and the people returned after him only to spoil (2 Sam. 23:9, 10). It was an often-repeated admonition in the Scriptures that men should arise. Unfortunately, throughout scriptures and in contemporary times, not many men and women have appeared to have obeyed this clarion call. Why is it that only very few dare hold the bull of their generation by the horn?

Eleazar rose from obscurity into relevance. He had a seemingly poor background, but he did not hesitate to strive toward a glorious future. He rose from nothing to something and from zero to hero. His father was a nobody, but his fortitude brought his father's name into God's book of record. His father was not an Israelite, but that was not an excuse for a man who determined to excel in life. He believed his potentials were more important and of higher value than the privileges he didn't have. He did something of eternal relevance with his talent. He invested his treasure in a noble and worthy cause. Can you be such a person in your day? Can you rise to join the class of those who will not succumb to the prevailing circumstances around their race, face, or pace as an excuse for mediocrity? Anyone with the spiritual make-up of Eleazar will undoubtedly become great in life, no matter the hurdles that men hurl at them on their way to the top.

Noteworthily, until Deborah arose a mother in Israel, the inhabitants of the villages ceased to follow their calling in Israel. Until David emerged on the battlefield to bring down Goliath, Israel continued to flee from their enemies. Until Saul, who later became Paul arose an apostle, not just among the Christian Jews, but as the sent-one to the Gentile world, Christ was not satisfied.

Today, the Philistines ravaging churches and denominations are not physical. We are currently at a time in church history when God needs men and women who would arise to speak and stand against the tide and trend of evil that is evolving in our generation. God needs men to arise and oppose satanic operations, dogmas that are being celebrated as theological exegesis, and denominational traditions that are being taught as biblical doctrines. The kingdom of Christ is being ravaged of the fruits of the ripened harvest of souls in many nations of the world. Can

God depend on you to arise against any of these tides? Would you be willing to arise when no one is there to stand with you? When will you arise, if not now?

He was a man who could smite the Philistines

*He arose, **and smote the Philistines until his hand was weary**, and his hand clave unto the sword: and the Lord wrought a great victory that day; and the people returned after him only to spoil* (2 Sam. 23:9, 10).

Not many have what it takes to smite the Philistines. As a leader, when you find such men who would stand with you to confront any challenge that comes your way, do not trivialize your relationship with them. The capacity to smite the adversary of the Lord is not a virtue that you can find in many people around the world. Wherever you find such men, either in the business, politics, or the church, do not ignore them.

There are leaders who knew that certain people should not be workers in the church of God, but they would still allow them to continue to serve because they wouldn't want to have a problem with anyone. They prefer to enjoy the smooth ride of ministry and administrative protocols to the detriment of God's work. The rampancy of carnal competition among ministers who ought to consolidate one another's gifts and the increasing domination of sinful practices that is evident in various denominations around the world further points to the reasons why revival has been delayed. It is quite apparent that some churches may never recover their good old days except there is a practical demonstration of genuine repentance and conscious purging on the pulpits and within the pews. *If my people, which are called by my name, shall humble themselves, and pray, and seek my face, and turn from their wicked ways; then will I hear from heaven, and will forgive their sin, and will heal their land* (2 Chron. 7:14).

Who will smite the giants of our time? It takes a person who can firmly stand on biblical standards to set these enemies on the run. Anyone who cannot confront the lion and the bear should have no business interacting with the governance of the flock.

He was a man who would not remove his hand from the sword in weariness

He arose, and smote the Philistines **until his hand was weary, and his hand clave unto the sword:** *and the Lord wrought a great victory that day; and the people returned after him only to spoil* (2 Sam. 23:9, 10).

This is another criterion that God looks for in leadership. At the point when many broke down or gave up, Eleazar continued to thrive. He changed from effort to skill. When your hand cleaves to the sword, your enemies are smitten effortlessly and with less energy. Not many people would go beyond the point of weariness. Only a skillful leader knows how to continue when the days are dreary and weary. However, if weariness sets in and the hand was not cleaved with the sword, the sword would fall. Today, it is crucial to master the use of the sword of the Spirit before the weary days come, during which efforts alone may not suffice.

When God tested Gideon's army, three hundred were faint, yet they pursued the enemies. These are the categories of men who would continue to fight in the face of every conceivable difficulty. Despite the multitudinous enemies that oppose the way of righteousness in the world, they would never give up. They are the sort of men who would cause commotions and panic in the conscience, heart, and camp of the transgressors. These are the men who could do the job of awakening a formal but dead church from its slumber and sleep of death. Such men combine tact and efficiency.

He was a man through whom God could bring about great victory

He arose, and smote the Philistines until his hand was weary, and his hand clave unto the sword: **and the Lord wrought a great victory that day**; *and the people returned after him only to spoil* (2 Sam. 23:9, 10).

God is a jealous God. He would not share His glory with any man, and this is crucial in leadership. God doesn't commit great victories into the hand of an arrogant man. He would not be impatient to kill Goliath before the arrival of a man after His own heart.

But he giveth more grace. Wherefore he saith, God resisteth the proud, but giveth grace unto the humble (James 4:6).

Many churches are stagnant today because of this issue. God could postpone revival for years if He knew that men would take the glory to themselves. Sometimes it is God that is resisting you and not the devil. One of the attributes that God wants to see in a man in whose hand He would do great things is for such to be small in his own eyes.

And Samuel said, when thou wast little in thine own sight, wast thou not made the head of the tribes of Israel, and the Lord anointed thee king over Israel? (1 Sam. 15:17).

God's standard is the same in every age, and in addition to the many identifiable positive qualities evident in the life of Eleazar, he met this huge requirement also.

...And the people returned after him only to spoil

He arose, and smote the Philistines until his hand was weary, and his hand clave unto the sword: and the Lord wrought a great victory that day; **and the people returned after him only to spoil** (2 Sam. 23:9, 10).

This is the culmination of the transcript of this great warrior, a leader who labored alone only for everyone to return to come and enjoy the spoils. We don't have many such men anymore. He was not an empty barrel. Eleazar was the type of leader you could commit a task into his hand and go to sleep. When you return, you can be sure he would deliver above and beyond expectations. He is a perfect team-player and someone who could work excellently without a great deal of supervision. These are the manner of men heaven seeks to behold in Christian ministry today!

3. Shammah, the Son of Agee the Hararite

And after him was Shammah the son of Agee the Hararite. And the Philistines were gathered together into a troop, where was a piece of ground full of lentiles: and the people fled from the Philistines. But he stood in the midst of the ground, and defended it, and slew the Philistines: and the Lord wrought a great victory (2 Sam. 23:11, 12).

He stood in the midst of the ground and defended it.

He stood in the midst of the ground, and defended it, and slew the Philistines: and the Lord wrought a great victory (2 Sam. 23:11, 12).

Shammah was a man who fulfilled the essence and purpose for which he was born and named. The meaning of his name was "astonishment," and indeed, he astonished men in his generation and beyond. These are the men God is looking for to lead His army today, men who would not be wanting when duty or danger calls. Shammah was a defender of the heritage of Israel under his care. Without reinventing the wheel, here is another man who made a mark in the sand of time. He would not allow the enemy to take over the harvest of the land. Shammah was another alien who rose by diligence and hard work to the rank of an army general, even in a foreign land. He was a non-Israelite who became a *Milicia excelsa,* an Iroko Tree in the beautiful city of Jerusalem, a man who would put his life on the line for the salvation of the lives of men with whom he shared no pedigree. He took the costliest risk to ensure God's people were not put to shame. God would be pleased with such a leader who could put his dear life as a down payment for the service and defense of others. Such acts were of a considerable sacrifice!

A man who would defend another man's heritage is undoubtedly a good leader.

And if ye have not been faithful in that which is another man's, who shall give you that which is your own? (Luke 16:12).

Surely, a man who would lay down his life for a piece of ground full of lentils would undeniably be willing to pay a higher price for the souls of men. Many are rushing into ministry today for gain alone but would exit at the sight of any pain or rigor of leadership.

Shammah joined the category of men who demonstrated Christlikeness in leadership. Jesus said, "Greater love hath no man than this, that a man lay down his life for his friends" (John 15:13).

The actions of these mighty men speak so loudly that we need not hear from them to believe they were worth the highly esteemed positions they occupied. Friend, this is what leadership entails.

Looking at the requirements presented by the lives of these three mighty men, do you think you merit the seat upon which you are currently sitting as a leader in your church? It is easy to attend leadership meetings, but can you stand when the Philistines show up in the church? Will you be there when the adversaries of the Lord gather themselves together in troops against sound doctrine and salvation of sinners? This might be a good time for you to look inward and evaluate your ministry. What ground are you defending for God? How many Philistines have you slain since you joined the army of the Lord? Have you pondered in recent times on how you even became a leader? Is it because you are the oldest or first to arrive at the location? After many years of toiling, why is it that your head still lacks the needed oil? Why would God refuse to bring the victory during your lifetime? Is it not because you have refused to allow others to utilize their God-given potentials out of fear of losing your leadership seat? Do you deny others opportunities that would have brought them into the limelight? Don't be satisfied with only marking time on the position of leadership. You can be the anointed one.

Sometimes someone who recently joined a ministry may have the grace to do much more than those who have been around for many years. If any leader is not willing to pay the price, why would you deny or hinder those who are willing to pay the price of satisfying the longings in the heart of God?

On the other hand, many leaders claim to be praying to God for revival. However, when the men God has sent to help them do the work begin to bring the spoils, they are either disciplined, put at a disadvantage, or denied privileged tasks that could bring such men to the limelight.

When Jesus saw this, He cried,

> O Jerusalem, Jerusalem, thou that killest the prophets, and stonest them which are sent unto thee, how often would I have gathered thy children together, even as a hen gathereth her chickens under her wings, and ye would not! **Behold, your house is left unto you desolate** (Matt. 23:37, 38).

Every leader would need these three

And three of the thirty chief went down, and came to David in the harvest time unto the cave of Adullam: and the troop of the

Philistines pitched in the valley of Rephaim. And David was then in an hold, and the garrison of the Philistines was then in Bethlehem (2 Sam. 23:13, 14).

It was harvest time, but the enemies had besieged Bethlehem. Danger songs could be heard from the valley of Rephaim. Like many church leaders today, David was thirsty and perhaps very tired. He was in a fix, as he had no choice other than to remain in the stronghold.

He longed, and said, Oh that one would give me drink of the water of the well of Bethlehem, which is by the gate! (2 Sam. 23:15)

Many church leaders wish to win young people today. They long to see revival among the youth, but they do not have the wherewithal to make it happen. Unfortunately, when God sends such firebrands into some churches, they are either persecuted or silenced. This is one of the reasons why several youths who are on fire for God look elsewhere, outside the local churches where they have been raised, to find fulfillment for their God-given potentials. It is sad to note that the innovative ideas (*which do not compromise God's Word and standards*), that young people bring to the table are considered "heresies" or "strange fires" by the same leaders who claim to be praying for revival.

These three men came to David without any invitation. They could sense their leader's need at such a critical period of his life. David knew he could not break through the host at this time to fetch the water from Bethlehem. At such a critical moment, God sent these three men, as an answer to the longing of David's heart.

Together, they broke through the host

And the three mighty men brake through the host of the Philistines, and drew water out of the well of Bethlehem, that was by the gate, and took it, and brought it to David (2 Sam. 23:16a).

These men broke through the host of the enemies strategically, drew the water, and brought it to their master.

Do you know that God is seeking for such men and women to stand in the gap? Like David, God is thirsty for souls today, and He will not be satisfied until the able, anointed ones are allowed to fulfill the calling of God upon their lives in the body of Christ.

Put the round pegs in round holes

For various reasons, David could have hindered them. If he did, two things might have happened. **One,** he might have gone for the water by himself, and he might have been killed or returned wounded, but as a good soldier, he stayed within his limits.

On the other hand, if he had considered that people would mock that it was these "three men" who rescued him, he would have died of thirst, and also hindered "these three mighty men from doing the great work that God had prepared them to accomplish for His kingdom, and a crucial victory would have been missed in God's kingdom.

As a leader, you need to pray to the Lord of the harvest to add such men and women, boys and girls, who can understand your challenges even before you tell them. Your ministry needs such people who would show up as the answer to your long-term prayers and desires. You need persons who will help you move the unmoved mountains and get done the work, which has remained undone for many years. To be successful, you need folks who could leave everything to answer the Master's call. Every organization needs such individuals, and divine wisdom is necessary to lead and handle them.

In every age, leaders who managed such men well have always accomplished great tasks for God. Every church must cherish and preserve them, whether they are among the youths or young adults. You must allow them to manifest the gifts and grace of God upon their lives, unless you are satisfied with the condition of your ministry.

REFLECTIONS ON CHAPTER TWO

The following questions may be used for personal reflections or group discussions:

1. What does God look for in those leading in His house?

i.

_____

ii.

_____

iii.

_____

iv.

_____

2. What do you look for in men you appoint?

i.

_____

ii.

_____

iii.

_____

iv.

_____

3. Who are the majority in your church's workforce? Are they adders, subtracters, dividers, or multipliers?

i.

_____

4. How many mighty men can you say are standing with you in what you are going through?

i. _____

ii. _____

iii. _____

iv. _____

5. How many adders and multipliers do you have as close companions?

i. Adders: _____

ii. Multipliers: _____

6. How many of the appointed are truly anointed by God for the work they are doing in your church?

i. _____

7. What ministry gifts are missing in your ministry? Are you ready to pay the price to obtain them?

_____

_____

_____

_____

THREE

FROM ABISHAI TO URIAH

A Synopsis of What God Does with Mighty Men

*These be the names of the **mighty men** whom David had...* (2 Sam. 23:8a)

Now, as we delve into the rest of the historical narrative of the other mighty men of David, it is necessary to define who a mighty man is. This all-important definition will necessarily depend on who is speaking. A man who sees himself as grasshopper would call the weakest of men a giant! Even an ordinary man could be referred to as a giant by a man who sees himself as a grasshopper!

I will like you to reflect sincerely and evaluate the manner and caliber of people who are singing your praises. Reflect on who is calling you great, and also check those who you call great. Do not be quick to answer. You must be sure you are not responding to the voice of the grasshoppers of this world. If grasshoppers are calling you great, be careful not to be deceived. On the other hand, if you see yourself as a grasshopper, the person you call great maybe a weakling in the chain of God's servants.

It is even more shocking that a church would ordain men in the class and colors of grasshoppers, and place great titles upon them and further saddle them with the job description of giants. This is what happens when a man becomes an overseer, pastor, teacher, apostle, or bishop without the requisite anointing and baptism of the Holy Ghost. While it is a known fact that God calls the unqualified, the truth remains that neither God nor Jesus sent any man on the field of souls without equipping them. For any meaningful work in the kingdom of God, genuine experiences of salvation, sanctification, and spirit baptism must be present in the minister's life.

God's work is not an easy task; neither is it an employment for the unstable in heart and devotion. God's requirement has not changed. Even in the Old Testament, the prerequisite standard was clear.

*Moreover thou shalt provide out of all the **people able men, such as fear God, men of truth, hating covetousness; and place such over them, to be rulers** of thousands, and rulers of hundreds, rulers of fifties, and rulers of tens:... and Moses chose able men out of all Israel, **and made them heads over the people,** rulers of thousands, rulers of hundreds, rulers of fifties, and rulers of tens* (Exod. 18:21, 25).

And in the New Testament, we read that "...*they chose Stephen, **a man full of faith and of the Holy Ghost,** ...* (Acts 6:5).

This is God-approved pattern, and when we follow it, the results are always evident.

And the word of God increased; and the number of the disciples multiplied in Jerusalem greatly; and a great company of the priests were obedient to the faith (Acts 6:7).

It would be unscriptural to think this is to be a requirement for specific denominations or a condition for churches in some uncivilized nations of the world. It is the divine requirement for the body of Christ in every culture and nation.

Genuinely mighty men have become endangered species, if not extinct in many churches. We are in an era in church history when "mighty men" are disadvantaged and disciplined while weaklings occupy great seats in the congregations. Perhaps, this explains why many denominations and churches are jam-packed with grasshopper believers in our days. What manner of disciples fill churches today? What shall we say when we have thirty churches in a city but not one evangelist? A church of fifty without a single prophet! A committee of seven without anyone to demonstrate the gifts of discernment and the word of knowledge. Does this not resemble the grasshoppers among the Israelitish spies?

The sad truth is before us—Many Christians in the body of Christ are no better than the spies that we read about during Moses' time. Grasshopper believers are Christians who exalt the enemies more than the power of their God. They are easily intimidated and afraid at the sight of the demoniac. To such, making heaven is not yet a matter of life and death. They could easily trade eternity for the comfort and cucumbers of Egypt. Unlike the catalog of mighty men written for our admonition in the inspired book of Hebrews, many of today's Christians would rather return to Egypt or die in the wilderness than fight their way into the everlasting presence of God. At best, such are not better than unbelievers as they do not believe that our heavenly Father has prepared a better place for them. Hence, they give up at the slightest resistance of foes. They have neither believed in the promise of Scriptures nor in themselves. Their confession was recorded for all ages to read and ponder on.

*But the men who went up with him said, **we be not able** to go up against the people; for they are stronger than we* (Num. 13:31).

David was a mighty man by many standards. This was not just the opinion of men; neither was it a kind of appellation culled from observation of his life and character. David's great-ness and might was a remarkable acknowledgment, articulated by God.

...I have found David the son of Jesse, **a man after mine own heart**, *which shall fulfil all my will* (Acts 13:22).

This is one of the most significant testimonies of any mortal man. Many men are called great, but not many have the strength and capacity to do **all the will of God.**

It is a notable attribute of great men to recognize the greatness in other men. Since this list of mighty men were either dictated or written by David, then each one of these men must be mighty indeed for David to call them so. Find out who are the majority in your congregation—grasshoppers or giant-killers?

The directory and description of David's mighty men

These be the names of the mighty men whom David had... (2 Sam. 23:8a)

Aside from the fact that the Bible didn't give so many details about the individual biographies of these mighty warriors, the little we read about them cannot be exhausted. They continue to present life challenges and admonitions to the generations coming after them. They teamed up to form an army that didn't lose any war in their lifetime. To become a member of this group of soldiers, a man had to show unparalleled deftness in warfare, unwavering courage in battle, and erudite sagacity in leadership. It is no doubt a cluster of mighty men whose lives continue to speak long after they are gone.

A cursory perusal of the list presents thirty-seven names grouped into three ranks, of which Uriah was last. It appears by their arrangement that these names were recorded according to their order of strength. Uriah might have also been mentioned last as the Holy Spirit's conviction wouldn't let David rest until he had cited Uriah's name. Notably, Joab's name appeared three times, but it was never to be for his recognition! This conspicuous omission is an issue that I will like you to meditate upon in the last chapter of this book. If Uriah was the least of all, then it further attests to the mightiness of these true, reliable, and faithful heroes of faith.

According to 2 Samuel 23, these are the names of the mighty men whom David had:

1. The Tachmonite, that sat in the seat, chief among the captains; the same was Adino the Eznite:

   - he *lifted* up his spear against eight hundred, whom he slew at one time.

2. Eleazar the son of Dodo the Ahohite, one of the three mighty men with David,

   - when they defied the Philistines that were there gathered together to battle, and the men of Israel were gone away: He arose, and smote the Philistines until his hand was weary, and his hand clave unto the sword: and the LORD wrought a great victory that day; and the people returned after him only to spoil.

3. Shammah the son of Agee the Hararite.

   - And the Philistines were gathered together into a troop, where was a piece of ground full of lentiles: and the people fled from the Philistines. But he stood in the midst of the ground, and defended it, and slew the Philistines: and the LORD wrought a great victory.

   - And three (*listed above*) of the thirty chief went down, and came to David in the harvest time unto the cave of

Adullam: and the troop of the Philistines pitched in the valley of Rephaim.

- And David was then in an hold, and the garrison of the Philistines was then in Bethlehem. And David longed, and said, Oh that one would give me drink of the water of the well of Bethlehem, which is by the gate!

- And the three mighty men brake through the host of the Philistines, and drew water out of the well of Bethlehem, that was by the gate, and took it, and brought it to David: nevertheless he would not drink thereof, but poured it out unto the LORD. And he said, Be it far from me, O LORD, that I should do this: is not this the blood of the men who went in jeopardy of their lives? therefore he would not drink it.

- These things did these three mighty men.

4. Abishai, the brother of Joab, the son of Zeruiah, was chief among three.

- And he lifted up his spear against three hundred, and slew them, and had the name among three.

- Was he not most honourable of three? therefore he was their captain: howbeit he attained not unto the first three.

5. Benaiah the son of Jehoiada, the son of a valiant man, of Kabzeel,

- who had done many acts, he slew two lionlike men of Moab:

- he went down also and slew a lion in the midst of a pit in time of snow:

- he slew an Egyptian, a goodly man: and the Egyptian had a spear in his hand; but he went down to him with a staff, and plucked the spear out of the Egyptian's hand, and slew him with his own spear.

- These things did Benaiah the son of Jehoiada; and had the name among three mighty men.

- He was more honorable than the thirty, but he attained not to the first three.

- David set him over his guard.

6. Asahel, the brother of Joab was one of the thirty;

7. Elhanan the son of Dodo of Bethlehem,

8. Shammah the Harodite,

9. Elika the Harodite,

10. Helez the Paltite,

11. Ira the son of Ikkesh the Tekoite,

12. Abiezer the Anethothite,

13. Mebunnai the Hushathite,

14. Zalmon the Ahohite,

15. Maharai the Netophathite,

16. the son of Baanah, a Netophathite,

17. Ittai the son of Ribai out of Gibeah of the children of Benjamin,

18. Benaiah the Pirathonite,

19. Hiddai of the brooks of Gaash,

20. Abialbon the Arbathite,

21. Azmaveth the Barhumite,

22. Eliahba the Shaalbonite, of the sons of Jashen,

23. Jonathan,

24. Shammah the Hararite,

25. Ahiam the son of Sharar the Hararite,

26. Eliphelet the son of Ahasbai,

27. the son of the Maachathite,

28. Eliam, the son of Ahithophel the Gilonite,

29. Hezrai the Carmelite,

30. Paarai the Arbite,

31. Igal the son of Nathan of Zobah,

32. Bani the Gadite,

33. Zelek the Ammonite,

34. Nahari the Beerothite, armourbearer to Joab the son of Zeruiah,

35. Ira an Ithrite,

36. Gareb an Ithrite,

37. Uriah the Hittite: thirty and seven in all.

Since all these men have several attributes in common, let us focus on the life of the seemingly least of them—Uriah, as a model and reference for them all. Each gleaning, through from the life of Uriah, would apply to all.

The description: distressed, in debt, and discontented

*David therefore departed thence, and escaped to the cave Adullam: and when his brethren and all his father's house heard it, they went down thither to him. And **every one that was in distress,** and **every one that was in debt,** and **every one that was discontented,** gathered themselves unto him; **and he became a captain over them:** and there were with him about four hundred men* (1 Sam. 22:1,2).

Though some were David's relatives, the majority by their names were outcasts of society.

While it is true that these men who surrounded David had notable problems, their dispositions toward life and attitudes in distress positioned them otherwise. Reflecting on the words of Apostle Paul: *I am debtor both to the Greeks, and to the Barbarians; both to the wise, and to the unwise* (Rom. 1:14).

The attitude of Uriah showed his indebtedness to his generation. His fortitude confirms that he was distressed with the comfort of the king's palace, and obviously, he was discontented with the continual reveling of the Philistines. He made up his mind to fight the good fight until the end. The path to greatness is marked by indebtedness, distress, and discontentment.

Until a man feels his indebtedness toward God and humanity, he may never do anything worthwhile with his life, talents, and resources of heaven at his disposal. This is what happened to men who lay down their lives for others. David rose to the challenge because he became sick of allowing God to be misrepresented. He became distressed at the sight of Goliath, felt indebted to the God of Israel, and discontented seeing the army of God hiding at the valley of Elah for a space of forty days, as a heathen from Gath bragged away. Obviously, David had reproduced himself in the mighty men, and it is quite noticeable around us today that only those who feel distressed about the mess going on in the name of Christ, and who feel indebted to the body of Christ and dissatisfied with the status quo would dare to make a mark in the sand of time. No life can be better spent, except it is well invested in God.

As it is written, *For David*, **after he had served his own generation by the will of God**, *fell on sleep, and was laid unto his fathers, and saw corruption* (Acts 13:36).

Like David, these men too served their generation before they left this world. In contemporary times, the people who have affected or who are making life-changing impacts began at their points of distress, indebtedness, and discontentment.

Some men made a difference because they became indebted to their generation. They became distressed and discontented with a poverty-stricken gospel. Many of God's generals became indebted to their generation. They became distressed and discontented with the propagation of a powerless gospel message before they did something that continues to live long after they are gone home. The distress and discontentment of one man, Martin Luther—with the religious leaders of his day and his undying feeling of indebtedness to Christ—gave birth to all the Protestant movement of our day.

In recent times, we are also seeing men who became indebted to their generation. Others got distressed and discontented with the pursuit of academic glory to obtain a degree with God. The distress, indebtedness, and discontentment of these men have won for them princely titles to gird not only them, but generations coming after them for the right. They have proved themselves a chosen race! Their stories and testimonies continue to draw men nearer unto their God.

The background of these mighty men

*And I will send hornets before thee, which shall drive out the Hivite, the Canaanite, **and the Hittite**, from before thee* (Exod. 23:28).

Like Uriah the Hittite, many of these mighty men were not Israelites. For example, the Hittites were the descendants of Heth, the second son of Canaan, who by their ancestry, were not to be part of God's program for the Israelites. They were part of the idolatrous nations that God drove out of the promised land. The question then comes to mind—how did Uriah and several others realign their destiny back to God?

First, the fact that many of their parents and grandparents were alienated from God, yet these ones found grace to be saved, tells much of the infinite mercy of God to those who would seek after Him. Second, it precludes all men from giving any reason for which they remain unsaved. If these ones who were disadvantaged could be brought into the purpose of God, there is no excuse for anyone who remained unsaved. Third, their lives continue to testify that to be conceived or born in sin should not be a justification for continuing in sin.

They would not accept a *mess* for a gift, even if it were to be from the king.

*And David said to Uriah, go down to thy house, and wash thy feet. And Uriah departed out of the king's house, **and there followed him a mess of meat from the king.** But Uriah slept at the door of the king's house with all the servants of his lord, and went not down to his house* (2 Sam. 11:8, 9).

Here was that low moment in the life of David. He had committed the sin of adultery with Uriah's wife. In a very shrewd and cruel attempt to make Uriah go home into his wife so that his heinous sin could go undiscovered, he followed up his persuasion with a mischievous mess of meat. However, Uriah was not of those who are given to change, even though Uriah's house is near enough to the king's palace for David to have seen Bathsheba bathing. Perhaps Bathsheba was one of the most beautiful in Israel, and having been away for weeks or months, the natural expectation was to go home and have a pleasant time with his wife. Uriah was of the stock of godly men who would not yield to the mess from the kings of this world. He could discern the smell of a mess in every tempting offer. He would rather sleep faithfully in the cold with the servants at the king's gate than to enjoy the warmth of his good-looking wife and the cozy comfort of his home.

How many men and women have lost their focus in ministry just because of a messy offer which came to them in the currency of position, promise, privilege, or pay. This is not unlike the man of God from Judah, who turned back to eat a meal of compromise, which led to the untimely ruin of his physical and spiritual destiny.

Uriah, though manipulated by the king into a state of stupor, would not allow his garment to be soiled! He was so disciplined that even though he was made drunk, he remained conscious of God! His deep-rooted morals were too strong for the momentary influence of strong drink. What manner of men are these? Like the scarceness of a virtuous woman, would Christ find such men in ministry when He returns?

They had their adversities but were not of little strength

If thou faint in the day of adversity, thy strength is small (Prov. 24:10).

Little was known about their marriages, but the little we knew about Uriah's wife speaks volumes that we could hear in every dispensation. Uriah was a man who would not allow his love for his wife to separate him from his commitment to God.

In comparison with Uriah, Bathsheba appeared to be of a lower consecration. It seems she was not compatible with the focus and dedication of her husband. Also noteworthy on the list of these great men was Bathsheba's father, Eliam, the son of Ahithophel. The two greatest men in her life—both her father and her dear husband—were at the war front! Rather than standing in the gap in prayers for their victory, she was busy compromising and messing on the lap of sin, with a man who was almost the age of her father. There was no record that she ever resisted the sinful allurement from the king, like her husband resisted until his blood was shed to the point of death. Neither was there a hint in scripture that she reported what happened between herself and David to her grandfather, Ahithophel, who was David's chief counselor. Even when she realized that she had become pregnant for her husband's boss, the scripture had no record of her being remorseful. Instead, she sent and told the king who, in turn, began to scheme how to cover their sins. Both David and Bathsheba knew that adultery carried a death penalty.

And the man who committeth adultery with another man's wife, even he that committeth adultery with his neighbor's wife, the adulterer and the adulteress shall surely be put to death (Lev. 20:10).

Perhaps Bathsheba was counting on David to shield her from the obvious consequence. This was the reason why Uriah was brought back from the battlefield. The plan was that he would be with his wife, and the child would become Uriah's. The scheming was perfected to cover David and Bathsheba's sin, a plot that eventually failed, leading to the deaths of an innocent child and a faithful husband.

David was indeed careless; nevertheless, a woman who could wreck the general of these mighty men should be greatly feared. Somehow, David was sure that Bathsheba would not confess their sin to her husband! Such women are too cheap for the price that heaven places upon the lives of God's mighty men. Today's soldiers of the cross must be wary of them as they are still very much around in the churches. It is not all so-called *born-again* brothers or sisters who are marriageable! There are even tongue-talking fornicators today! A word is enough for the wise and discerning: *Let not thine heart decline to her ways, go not astray in her paths. For she hath cast down many wounded: yea, many strong men have been slain by her. Her house is the way to hell, going down to the chambers of death* (Prov. 7:25–27).

Like many in various churches today, Bathsheba was keener to perform the duties of ceremonial law than the moral laws of God. She was passionate about purifying herself from the uncleanness of her menses than seeking the face of God for the cleansing of her sinful heart.

And David sent messengers, and took her; and she came in unto him, and he lay with her; for she was purified from her uncleanness: and she returned unto her house (2 Sam. 11:4). Does this not depict the lives of many preachers today? Those who are preaching holiness when their hearts are full of rot. Some are disciplining other people's children while their own children are becoming twice the children of hell under their roof? It is like the Pharisees whom Jesus rebuked. *Howbeit in vain do they worship me, teaching for doctrines the commandments of men. For laying aside the commandment of God, ye hold the tradition of men, as the washing of pots and cups: and many other such like things ye do* (Mark 7:7–8).

I am wondering how Bathsheba entered into the life of such a faithful man. Those who are on a journey with God must take their marriages seriously.

They fulfilled New Testament criteria in the Old Testament

And every one that hath forsaken houses, or brethren, or sisters, or father, or mother, or wife, or children, or lands, for my name's sake, shall receive an hundredfold, and shall inherit everlasting life (Matt. 19:29).

Uriah, like a few others, went ahead of the New Testament saints to forsake houses, or brethren, or sisters, or father, or mother, or wife, or children, or lands, for the sake of God's name. These men were positioned to receive a hundredfold with persecutions in this life and in the world to come, eternal life (Matt. 19:29; Mark 10:29, 30). This is an issue that many are still struggling with today. Some people want to be in the world and at the same time, in the church. Many leaders are compromising to remain in their comfort zone and wishing to eat the spoils of war.

Eliam, who was Ahithophel's son and father of Bathsheba, remained loyal in the army of Israel, despite David's infidelity and unfaithfulness. These men knew their battles were for God's glory and not just for David's kingdom. Even when Ahithophel defected with David's son—Absalom—to conspire against David, these men, including the missing Joab, (whose matter shall be covered in later chapters), maintained their loyalty unto David. Having loved David and God's calling upon him, they all loved him until the end.

They were men of Christlike passion

When Jesus knew that his hour was come that he should depart out of this world unto the Father, having loved his own which were in the world, he loved them unto the end (John 13:1).

Like our Lord and Savior Jesus Christ, all these mighty men lay down their lives for their brethren, king, and the glory of their God. In every battle, they fought until victory was won; they were loyal in their calling unto the end. They all shared the same passion wherever they were. As others were fighting for God's heritage, Uriah was resisting the pressure of the king to compromise his precious values. These are the needed men in the body of Christ today. Men who would go all the way to pay the price for the salvation of souls and ensure that God's purpose is eternally engraved upon the hearts of men.

Uriah was mindful of his assignment. Though, distracted from the field, his heart was fixed on his duty post. The obvious backsliding of the king would not deter his commitment to the Lord. In Uriah, we see a man who would sleep at the door of the king's house with all the servants of his lord.

> *And when they had told David, saying, Uriah went not down unto his house, David said unto Uriah, Camest thou not from thy journey? why then didst thou not go down unto thine house? And Uriah said unto David, The ark, and Israel, and Judah, abide in tents; and my lord Joab, and the servants of my lord, are encamped in the open fields; shall I then go into mine house, to eat and to drink, and to lie with my wife? as thou livest, and as thy soul liveth, I will not do this thing. And David said to Uriah, Tarry here to day also, and to morrow I will let thee depart. So Uriah abode in Jerusalem that day, and the morrow.*

> *And when David had called him, he did eat and drink before him; and he made him drunk: and at even he went out to lie on his bed with the servants*

of his lord, but went not down to his house. And it came to pass in the morning, that David wrote a letter to Joab, and sent it by the hand of Uriah.

And he wrote in the letter, saying, set ye Uriah in the forefront of the hottest battle, and retire ye from him, that he may be smitten, and die (2 Sam. 11:10–15).

Like Jesus, Uriah overcame all the odds and temptations that cripple men today; he was allured with sex and he overcame. He triumphed over all the fiery darts of the enemy hurled at his soul. Though childless, he would not go in unto his wife at the hour when he should be combating the enemy of his God.

He was severely pushed to feel highly exalted as the king arranged an entourage of mess to escort him into compromise. Rather, Uriah joined the men of low estate at the king's gate. He was tempted to be disrespectful, even when the king deserved a rebuke, but he would not rebuke his king. After three days of hard resistance, Uriah passed his penultimate test of love for God. He took his own death sentence and traveled his last mile of the way. He went back to duty, to die and to win. His faithfulness was put to the test, but he would not yield as he refused to open the letter on the way.

Their lives were centered on God

And Uriah said unto David, The ark, and Israel, and Judah, abide in tents; and my lord Joab, and the servants of my lord, are encamped in the open fields; shall I then go into mine house, to eat and to drink, and to lie with my wife? as thou livest, and as thy soul liveth, I will not do this thing (2 Sam. 11:11).

Again, in the least of David's mighty men, we see a man who loved and feared God above his backsliding commander. He would not be a partaker in other men's sins. Uriah mirrored Christ by suffering cruel betrayal from those he loved the most—Joab and David. He was sacrificed for the sins of others. He manifested Christlike grace in the most unlikely moment. This also refutes the claim that a leader's sin is a leading sin. Sin is a choice. If you don't want to do it, no man can force it on you. Joseph was tempted, but he refused because he saw sin as wickedness against God. Job would not sin, even when the wife suggested it. Daniel refused to be defiled by the king's meat and wine. Mordecai, at the risk of his life, stood against the reigning evil in the palace of King Ahasuerus, and he outlived the son of perdition. Likewise, the three Hebrew children stood in the fire, and the fire had no power over them.

David's men would not lose sight of the battle of the Lord, even when their king had temporarily lost his hold and love for God.

They were God's lights in their generation

> *Ye are the light of the world ... let your light so shine before men, that they may see your good works, and glorify your Father which is in heaven* (Matt. 5:14–16).

Etymologically, **Uriah means the "light of God,"** and like the other mighty men, he lived up to his name.

Latently seated in David's morals was a weakness toward women. For a long time, this remained invisible to the public eye and undiscovered, probably due to his astute cleverness and military exploits, until Uriah's uncompromising moral life helped shed the divine light of God upon this dark side of

David's life. Had Uriah gone home to spend the night with his wife, David's sin would have gone undiscovered.

Aside from the fact that David loved God with all his heart, his heart for women remained a major problem. Recall what he did the moment he heard that King Saul would give his daughter to the man who kills the giant.

> *And the men of Israel said, Have ye seen this man that is come up? surely to defy Israel is he come up: and it shall be, that the man who killeth him, the king will enrich him with great riches, and will give him his daughter, and make his father's house free in Israel. And David spake to the men that stood by him, saying, what shall be done to the man that killeth this Philistine, and taketh away the reproach from Israel? for who is this uncircumcised Philistine, that he should defy the armies of the living God? And the people answered him after this manner, saying, So shall it be done to the man that killeth him* (1Sam. 17:25, 26).

When he was to pay the dowry, it is unbelievable how David risked his life again just in an attempt to marry a girl who would eventually be a snare unto his life. Like Samson, it appears David would do anything when it comes to the matter of women. Who would have discovered this dark side of David's moral life?

And when the wife of Uriah heard that Uriah her husband was dead, she mourned for her husband. And when the mourning was past, David sent and fetched her to his house, and she became his wife, and bare him a son. But the thing that David had done displeased the Lord (2 Sam. 11:26, 27).

This deficiency and moral weakness also manifested itself in David's life immediately he heard of Nabal's demise. *And when David heard that Nabal was dead, he said, Blessed be the Lord, that hath pleaded the cause of my reproach from the hand of Nabal, and hath kept his servant from evil: for the Lord hath returned the wickedness of Nabal upon his own head. And David sent and communed with Abigail, to take her to him to wife* (1 Sam. 25:39).

It was Uriah's life that eventually served as God's instrument for David's redemption as it helped to shine the divine light on the darkness in David's life, which led to David's repentance, redemption, and restoration. Like our Lord Jesus Christ, Uriah, died the death of the righteous, working out the salvation of David's soul.

Are you a hypocrite but wearing a Christian's garment or occupying a church leadership office? May God shed His light upon the dark side of your life even as read this book.

They were all faithful till death

Be thou faithful unto death, and I will give thee a crown of life (Rev. 2:10).

Uriah did not live to see the earthly fruits of his toiling, but **his faithfulness made room for him in the genealogy of Christ. He has been rewarded in the life that now is, and no man would take his crown in that which is to come.**

*And Jesse begat David the king; and David the king begat **Solomon of her that had been the wife of Urias*** (Matt. 1:6).

Thus, Uriah became a bonafide member of the unnamed Heroes of Faith (Heb. 11:39,40).

He traveled to his eternal reward, leaving a tremendous challenge for you and me. He was faithful until death.

If this is the summary of the life of the least on the list of these mighty men, where would those who are tagged mighty in many churches today be found?

REFLECTIONS ON CHAPTER THREE

The following questions may be used for personal reflections or group discussions:

1. Do you have some standard criteria for people who want to work in your church? If yes, list these criteria.

i. _____

ii. _____

iii. _____

iv. _____

v. _____

vi. _____

2. Do you keep a record of what each worker under you is doing? If yes, list each worker and review the criteria upon which each were chosen.

i. _____

ii. _____

iii.

_____

iv.

_____

v.

_____

3. How many Uriahs' lives have been cut short due to leader-ship manipulations in your ministry? List their names and ask God for direction on what to do about these ones.

i.

_____

ii.

_____

iii.

_____

iv.

_____

v.

_____

4. Are you guilty of using administrative moves to cover your sins or omissions? If yes, repent and set out time to do the necessary restitutions.

_____

_____

_____

5. Do you think the folks in your church are keener to perform ceremonial duties than the moral laws of God? If yes, ask God for corrective steps.

_____

_____

_____

6. What have you left behind for the sake of Christ that is of a
    great price to you?

i. _____

ii. _____

iii. _____

iv. _____

v. _____

7. What has been your reaction to corrections from subordi-
    nates and younger fellows?

i. _____

ii. _____

iii. _____

iv. _____

v. _____

FOUR

HARVEST

Critical Moments in a Man's Life

*And three of the thirty chief went down, and came to David **in the harvest time** unto the cave of Adullam: and the troop of the Philistines pitched in the valley of Rephaim*
(2 Sam. 23:13).

The harvest time is a critical period in the affairs of nations, people, families, and individuals. It is an era that God, Satan, and humanity look forward to. All through scriptures, the truth about harvest is replete. As shown in the passage above, harvest time is a time usually targeted by the enemy. For various reasons, it is crucial and instructive for you to reflect on how this applies to you. The enemy may be coming after your season of harvest or that of your ministry, family, or nation. Particularly, you need to be aware of what is going on in the spirit realm about the season of harvest in your life.

Your harvest might be attracting the enemies

*And it shall be as **when the harvestman gathereth** the corn, and reapeth the ears with his arm; and it shall be as he that gathereth ears **in the valley of Rephaim** (Isaiah. 17:5).*

The valley of Rephaim is where the harvest was usually stored in Israel, and it is noteworthy that the enemy also pitched their troops in the valley of Rephaim. Over the years, the word *Rephaim* has been used to describe giants or an old tribe of giants. It is a thing of concern when the adversaries take over that which ought to bring joy and comfort. Apostle Paul wrote in his letter to the Corinthian church how the enemies increased following his impressive and successful breakthrough. *For a great door and effectual is opened unto me, and there are many adversaries* (1 Cor. 16:9).

During Gideon's time, the enemies always showed up at the time of harvest, and the same was David's experience. If this is what you are also experiencing, you must fight the good fight of faith.

> "(For the weapons of our warfare are not carnal, but mighty through God to the pulling down of strong holds;) casting down imaginations, and every high thing that exalteth itself against the knowledge of God, and bringing into captivity every thought to the obedience of Christ; and having in a readiness to revenge all disobedience, when your obedience is fulfilled" (2 Cor. 10:4).

You must steadfastly hold on to God. Trust Him, and be sure to live a holy life. Employ and deploy your weapon of warfare in the Lord against the stronghold of the adversary of your harvest. God is still on the throne. He will surely fight for you, and you will undoubtedly overcome.

Your season of harvest is a token of God's covenant with you

*While the earth remaineth, seedtime **and harvest**, and cold and heat, and summer and winter, and day and night shall not cease* (Gen. 8:22).

Many times, God makes covenants with several individuals. The point where the covenant is made could be considered as the seedtime, while the fulfillment of the promise or covenant becomes the harvest. In His dealings with man, God is always committed to His own side of every covenant. While the earth remains, your harvest will surely come. Has God promised you a harvest, but hope seems to be deferred? You need to hold on to His Word in faith and obedience. However, since the enemy cannot hinder the harvest that God has approved for an individual or an organization, including churches, he usually attempts to destroy the harvest, steal it, or kill it or the harvester so that God's kingdom might record a loss. As a believer, you must awaken to the reality of what is going on regarding the harvest that you so desire.

There are marriages with fertile seeds, but whose seeds always got aborted before the harvest time when the wife should have given birth. God does not want you to miscarry your young; Satan does. God's covenant with humanity is fruitfulness and not barrenness. You must anticipate your season of harvest, and if you don't see it in due time, the adversary may be at work. The harvest of several ministries is under attack today. Leaders are fighting one another while the enemy steals the fruits of the harvest. You might call it a misunderstanding, but in the spirit realm, it might be an attack. Every discerning mind should see that we are in the season of harvest that Jesus foretold. Unfortunately, the disunity in the body of Christ has never been so great. Satan attacks churches by creating disputes, unforgiveness, and disharmony among workers. Due to the strife among ministers of the gospel, many revival harvests are wasting away.

Harvest is the time when parents should eat the fruits of their labor on their children

*And Reuben went **in the days of wheat harvest,** and found mandrakes in the field, **and brought them unto his mother** Leah. Then Rachel said to Leah, give me, I pray thee, of thy son's mandrakes* (Gen. 30:14).

Every parent looks forward to the time when they can sit back and begin to eat the fruits of their labors over their children. This is the primary motivation for investing resources, time, and treasures in child training in many parts of the world. Especially where there is no reliable retirement package for the geriatrics, having good children is considered a necessary asset for the old age. I have not met a parent who is not looking forward to this. However, in many families, the enemy takes revenge on the parents by afflicting their children, thereby robbing them of the joy of harvest. If you have children, you must intentionally engage the enemy in prayers over their lives so that your joy may be full in old age.

Harvest is the time designed by God for you to feast

*And thou shalt observe the **feast** of weeks, of the firstfruits of wheat harvest, and the **feast** of ingathering at the year's end* (Exod. 23:16; 34:22).

Feasting is the opposite of fasting. It is synonymous to rest after labor. While it is not an everyday routine, it would be awful to go through life without feasting at least once. In God's program for His people, there are weeks that God has set apart for feasting. It is a period of ingathering and celebration. It is a celebration of harvest which also commemorates God's provision for His people. It is a remarkable reminder of His sustenance of His people.

When last did you feast? When was the last time that people came to celebrate something that God has done in your life? Beloved, you must realize that Satan does not want you to have this beautiful and comforting experience. If you are not experiencing regular seasons of celebration, it could be an indication that the enemy is besieging your harvest.

Harvest is a time designed for you to rest

*That which groweth of its own accord of thy harvest thou shalt not reap, neither gather the grapes of thy vine undressed: for **it is a year of rest** unto the land* (Lev. 25:5).

God wants all men to have a time of rest. However, the concept of rest goes beyond lying down upon the bed. Many people are restless on their beds due to nightmares, sicknesses, pains, and all sorts of troubles that came upon them. Many scientific researches and polls have confirmed this.

A 2005 report[1] shows that more than half of the people in America experienced at least one of the following more than once every week: difficulty falling asleep, waking up a lot during the night, waking up too early, and not being able to get back to sleep, or waking up feeling unrested, while thirty-three percent of the population said they had at least one of these symptoms every night or almost every night. In 2018, during the Annual Meeting of the Associated Professional Sleep Societies LLC (APSS), a study[2] also revealed that about 25 percent of Americans experience acute insomnia each year.

According to scriptures, *It is vain for you to rise up early, to sit up late, to eat the bread of sorrows: for **so he giveth his beloved sleep*** (Psalm 127:2).

Since God wants men to have a good sleep, it is essential to note that Satan may be the mastermind behind most of these sleeplessness encounters among men. Satan uses various tools at his disposal—sickness, pains, fears, and worries. Even though medical science attempts to diagnose every situation and give it a name, the believer must not be ignorant of the devices of the devil. In God's program, even the land is entitled to a season of rest. Your time of harvest is proverbially the time God has designed for you to rest. Unfortunately, Satan continues to interfere with God's plan for man.

Restlessness is more of a spiritual problem than a physical one. Perhaps, you have never experienced your ordained season of rest. You did business, and but when you were about to start to rest on the profits, something bad happened that swept them all away. Then you began to struggle again. Leaders experience this pattern in their ministries as well. Many people are not able to rest due to frustrations, troubles, and problems that continue to surface at the eleventh hour of their breakthrough. If this describes your very situation, do not trivialize it. It is an indication that you need prayer.

Harvest is the time to help the widows, needy, and orphans, and to feed the poor free of charge

*And **when ye reap the harvest of your land,** thou shalt not make clean riddance of the corners of thy field when thou reapest, neither shalt thou gather any gleaning of thy harvest: thou shalt leave them unto the poor, and to the stranger: I am the Lord your God (Lev. 23:22).*

When thou cuttest down thine harvest in thy field, *and hast forgot a sheaf in the field, thou shalt not go again to fetch it: it shall be for the stranger, for the fatherless, and for the widow: that the Lord thy God may bless thee in all the work of thine hands* (Deut. 24:19).

It is a command from the Lord to His people to remember the poor, widows, and orphans when they reap their harvest. Unfortunately, not many churches are contributing toward relieving the poor, widows, and fatherless today. Rather than help these people, many denominations have chosen to focus on building schools and hospitals that even most of their members could not afford.

In former times, churches built schools to evangelize communities, but today churches are establishing schools to make money! Even though these institutions are called Christian schools, the lives of the students who attend are far worse than their peers who attended the public schools. How did the church arrive at this point of decadence? While there are still a few churches that are being faithful to the Lord, the majority are only doing business in the name of Christ. Leaders should always reflect on the scripture. "Pure religion and undefiled before God and the Father is this, To visit the fatherless and widows in their affliction, and to keep himself unspotted from the world" (James 1:27).

The harvest period should be a time of Thanksgiving

Speak unto the children of Israel, and say unto them, When ye be come into the land which I give unto you, and shall reap the harvest thereof, then ye shall bring a sheaf of the firstfruits of your harvest unto the priest (Lev. 23:10).

The harvest period is supposed to be a time of showing gratitude to the Lord with the best that you have. It is not a time to take the glory for your successes and attainments. It is the best time to give the credit of your achievements to God, who gave you the power to make wealth. God is a jealous God, and if anyone robs Him of His glory, He will require it.

Thanksgiving has been observed officially in Canada since 1957. It was a day of giving thanks to God for the bountiful harvest He has given the people. However, this celebration had started in 1578, which was over 350 years before the Canadian governor general's proclamation, by the Northwest Passage explorers who gave thanks to God for surviving a long and dangerous voyage via the waterways of Canadian Arctic Archipelago.[3]

Over the years, Thanksgiving Day has been observed as a holiday to give thanks for the blessings in one's life, particularly the harvest. In the United States, Canada, and many other nations of the world, it comes with a day off work. At the outset of these celebrations, people gave thanks to God for their harvests in the passing year. There is no argument about this. **The histories of these nations confirm their giving of thanks to God.**

Today in many parts of the world, many nations are busy enjoying the divine rain and blessings of nature, but the Thanksgiving holiday is observed without giving any recognition to God. Recently, a Canadian woman was asked what the purpose of the Thanksgiving holiday is? In an attempt to skew God out of the equation, she said it is just a time to give thanks. When she was asked who would she thank? She said anyone could be appreciated!

Satan will fight anything that would make anyone give thanks to God. He has also blinded the eyes of men, so they do not recognize God in their lives. He wants to destroy humanity. Do not be fooled to arrogate your success to your skills and talents or to think you or someone is responsible for your success.

The next time you experience any form of harvest/success, do not forget to give the glory unto God by bringing Him the first-fruits of your thanksgiving.

Harvest is a time when riches increase and over-flows the banks

And as they that bare the ark were come unto Jordan, and the feet of the priests that bare the ark were dipped in the brim of the water, ***(for Jordan overfloweth all his banks all the time of harvest)*** (Josh. 3:15).

Water has been referred to as a universal solvent, and this is not only true in chemistry; It is true in many facets of life. Water is a resource that affects many economic activities, and its availability or scarcity affects economic growth. It is necessary in almost every sector of the human economy. Generally, agriculture is more difficult without sufficient water in place. Its importance in livestock production, energy production, building construction, residential, domestic, food processing, and several other industrial demands proclaims the significance of water. When water is in short supply, it usually leads to food shortages and inflation of commodity prices, which in turn results in civil instability. The importance of water cannot be overemphasized in the economy of any nation. Historical authorities have it on good record that the ancient Egyptian civilization depended on the resources of the great river Nile, which has given rise to the phrase, "Egypt is the Nile, and the Nile Egypt." Indeed, the water of a nation contributes to her economic strength and wealth.

It is therefore noteworthy that the banks of Jordan always overflow in harvest. When you apply this scripture to an individual or a family, it implies God's desire is to have your riches increase beyond the banks during your harvest. Harvest therefore means a time when you have more than savings. Such time could be a time when someone has enough to spare and distribute to the necessities of others. It is, however, sad to note that not many people have this testimony of having enough to save, share and distribute. It is possible to go through life and never experience this form of harvest. The majority in various nations of the world are living from hand to mouth. Even in the developed world, many are living with multiple debts.

It should make you uncomfortable if you have nothing to share, distribute, or spare from your harvest. It is not pleasant to have less than you need for yourself when your salary (harvest) arrives. It is very distressing to have an appetite but have no food. It might even become more embarrassing when those who look up to you knock on your door to discover you are a well without water because you have nothing to offer. Such situation is quite contrary to God's expectation for you at the time of harvest. When your harvest comes, your water, which proverbially is a symbol of your wealth, ought to have increased to the extent that you could share and spare for those in need. If this is not your experience, you may need to seek divine wisdom or work harder. You may also need to fight the enemy who may be working behind the scene.

It is wrong to be playing or sleeping at the time of harvest

But it came to pass within a while after, in the time of wheat harvest, that Samson visited his wife with a kid; and he said, I will go in to my wife into the chamber. But her father would not suffer him to go in (Judges 15:1)

The harvest is also a time of serious business, not a time to be loafing around. There is a good kind of sleep, but there is another kind that could lead to death.

Unfortunately, we see Samson, sleeping around with women during the time of harvest. His father tried to help him, but Samson would not listen. As Proverbs 10:5 states, "He that gathereth in summer is a wise son: but **he that sleepeth in harvest is a son that causeth shame**." When a man sleeps in the time of harvest, shame is inevitable. Samson brought a disgrace upon his calling and to the name of God. Following the errors of Samson's life, the proponents of eternal security have come to believe that they, too, can continue in sin while still operating in the grace of God. You must be awake to the reality of this era. It is harvest time, and if you are not busy for the Lord, you may be the sleeper in the time of harvest. Today, the enemy has hypnotized many believers, and if such sleep continues uninterrupted, it might end in the physical or spiritual death of those believers.

Jesus told us that the harvest is a time for every servant of the Lord to be up and doing something for the Lord. If you are not yet awake to the reality of soul-winning in this end time, you are either playing, sleeping, or straying away from the Lord. I pray this book awakens you to the realization of the harvest around you.

Harvest time is the right time to return to your Bethlehem

*So Naomi returned, and Ruth the Moabitess, her daughter in law, with her, which returned out of the country of Moab: and **they came to Bethlehem in the beginning of barley harvest*** (Ruth 1:22)

There must be something important about the season of harvest, which would explain why the enemy is very particular about it. The believer must not take his harvest for granted. It was the time of harvest when David was seeking for someone to break through the garrison of the Philistines to fetch him water to refresh his thirsty and distressed soul. The harvest was also a very timely moment in the life of Ruth and Naomi, as it was their time of return. To return to Bethlehem at the time of harvest seems to be a necessary move for any believer who has been away from the plan and purpose of God. Bethlehem, by interpretation, means the "house of bread."

Perhaps, you have been a believer for quite a while, but you can now sense the fire of God upon your life. Have you noticed that the profitability you used to experience is beginning to diminish or go down or has even vanished? Friend, you can make this season of kingdom harvest of souls your time of return to the God of your salvation so that He can feed you with the bread of heaven.

Harvest is a time of divine visitation

And they of Bethshemesh were reaping their wheat harvest in the valley: and they lifted up their eyes, and saw the ark, and rejoiced to see it, also, O Judah, he hath set an harvest for thee, when I returned the captivity of my people (1 Sam. 6:13; Hos. 6:11)

There are many seasons in the year—winter, spring, summer, and fall. I do not have an answer as to why God visited the Jews at the time of harvest. One notable allusion is evident from the incidences cited above. Even in the New Testament, the precedent continues among the Jews. The release of the promise of the Father upon the waiting disciples was at the period of their harvest.

When important personalities visit you, courtesy demands that you recognize and acknowledge them. It would be morally wrong not to acknowledge someone who has contributed positively to your success in life when occasion demands it. Hence,

I believe that a right attitude toward God in prayer and praises during your season of harvest will draw God closer to you. Let's consider an incidence in the Old Testament.

And Jethro, Moses' father in law, came with his sons and his wife unto Moses into the wilderness, where he encamped at the mount of God: and he said unto Moses, I thy father in law Jethro am come unto thee, and thy wife, and her two sons with her. **And Moses went out to meet his father in law, and did obeisance**, *and kissed him; and they asked each other of their welfare; and they came into the tent* (Exod. 18:5–7).

Jethro, Moses's spiritual mentor, came to visit Moses. Moses demonstrated maturity and a deep sense of morality by leaving whatsoever he was doing on the mount of God to recognize the visitation of his spiritual mentor and father-in-law. If Moses had not demonstrated a humble attitude at such a moment of divine visitation, he would have continued to weary himself and the people following him. Who would have thought that the counsel from Jethro, who didn't have a large congregation like Moses, would give birth to the concept of church leadership that has become a model for many churches worldwide today? Sometimes we lose much unknowingly, due to arrogance and disrespect for those who God has placed over us. If you remember God during your moments of increase, He would surely be motivated to visit you with more of His infinite blessings. Those who take God for granted when riches and ministry increase only set themselves up for subsequent divine disfavor. Be careful how you treat God when your harvest arrives or when your riches increase. In the case of the people of Bethshemesh, a divine visitation that would have brought them blessings resulted in tragedy because they did not reverence the presence of the Holy One.

Harvest could also be a divinely appointed time to measure judgment that comes to the wicked

*And he delivered them into the hands of the Gibeonites, and they hanged them in the hill before the Lord: and they fell all seven together, **and were put to death in the days of harvest,** in the first days, **in the beginning of barley harvest** (2 Sam. 21:9).*

For every act or deed sown, there shall be a harvest in return. Saul sowed the seeds of evil, hatred, oppression, and attempted the murder of the innocent and anointed on several occasions. He had the power, and he wielded it as he pleased. He practiced evil until he became proficient at his evil plots. He blatantly disregarded the law of God. In his hardness of heart, he unwittingly broke a three-hundred-year-old covenant that Israel had with the Gibeonites, and the outcome was grave.

*Then there was a famine in the days of David three years, year after year; and David enquired of the Lord. **And the Lord answered, it is for Saul, and for his bloody house, because he slew the Gibeonites** (2 Sam. 21:1).*

Saul departed from God and sold his heart to Satan. He drifted toward sin and became very wicked. But by the time harvest time came, he had to reap the consequences of his atrocious acts through the hanging of his progeny. Even in death, he did not escape. Covenant breakers in marriage, business, and those who are using their position to punish the innocent should remember that Satan might be pushing them toward a harvest of sorrow and regret. The enemy's mandate has never changed—to steal, kill, and destroy the season of harvest for those who follow him. On the other hand, God, who always avenges the innocent, did not spare Saul of divine judgment at the right time of harvest. For every covenant we keep or break, there awaits divine retribution for all men when God returns to harvest the earth.

Harvest is the time to gather food

Go to the ant, thou sluggard; consider her ways, and be wise: which having no guide, overseer, or ruler, provideth her meat in the summer, **and gathereth her food in the harvest** (Prov. 6:8).

Harvest is a time to gather food. Naturally, in many parts of the world, the fall and winter seasons immediately follow the season of harvest come. Both fall and winter seasons are quite unfavorable for work due to the inclement weather, at least for the ants. If you apply this to your life as a person, the harvest is the season of your life when you have the opportunity to do all the gatherings—save money, invest time, talents, and treasures in profitable ventures. Failure to do this is the reason why many people develop depressive tendencies later in life. If you do not gather food when you are young, you will have nothing to share in your old age. If you don't devour anything in the morning of your career, you may have no spoil to divide for your children in the evening of your life.

Benjamin shall ravin as a wolf: **in the morning he shall devour the prey,** *and* **at night he shall divide the spoil** (Gen. 49:27).

How old are you now? What can you say you have gathered? Scriptures tell us everyone has an average of seven to eight decades. *The days of our years are threescore years and ten; and if by reason of strength they be fourscore years, yet is their strength labor and sorrow; for it is soon cut off, and we fly away. So teach us to number our days, that we may apply our hearts unto wisdom* (Ps. 90:10, 12).

If you think in decades and not in years, you will realize you don't have many. In the same way, the harvest doesn't last forever; you will not always have the opportunity to gather in life.

Due to the various peculiarities that characterize the season of harvest, it requires much diligence and discipline not to eat your entire harvest all at once. This doesn't remove the need to give or share during your harvest. However, you must not share or give away that which should be invested or reserved into the barns. John Wesley's principle of *"earning all you can, giving all you can and saving all you can"* is an essential food for thought in this regard.[4]

When you apply these principles during your years of opportunities, you will gather much and become rich (Prov. 10:4, 5). It will make you prosperous, and several benefits would accrue to you (Prov. 12:11, 14). While others are wallowing in wants and troubles, you would be enjoying a comfortable life of abundance (Prov. 20:4).

A good harvest is a function of rain

*And also I have withholden the rain from you, **when there were yet three months to the harvest**: and I caused it to rain upon one city, and caused it not to rain upon another city: one piece was rained upon, and the piece whereupon it rained not withered* (Amos 4:7).

Let me reiterate that this is the season of harvest for the church, yet the need for rain cannot be overemphasized. You will agree that rain is always a prerequisite to a good harvest. As a minister, it is a waste of time to anticipate a harvest of souls when God has not sent rain upon your life. God must first send rain to soften the ground of their hearts for the entrance of His Word upon both the preacher and those who would hear him to yield any good results. It would be very frustrating to be laboring on a field that is devoid of divine rain. You would have been tired when only very little work had been done. Those laboring with you also would get weary when they labor only on dry ground. That is why you need to make it a personal priority to ensure heaven sends rain upon you before you start running around in ministry. However, if you want revival, you must heed the admonition of the Lord "who giveth rain upon the earth, and sends waters upon the fields" (Job 5:10). You would have to "sow to yourselves in righteousness, reap in mercy; break up your fallow ground: for it is time to **seek the Lord, till he come and rain righteousness upon you**" (Hos. 10:12).

The need for you to break every fallow ground of sinful habits in your life is crucial. In God's dealings with any man or congregation, repentance and righteousness are always prerequisite requirements for revival. Those who have ever obtained mercy from the Lord could attest to this.

Without enough laborers, the harvest will waste away

Then saith he unto his disciples, the harvest truly is plenteous, but the labourers are few; pray ye therefore the Lord of the harvest, that he will send forth labourers into his harvest (Matt. 9:37, 38).

Have you wondered why genuine laborers are very few in the time of harvest? Seven times in scripture, Jesus alluded to the harvest, using agricultural parables (Matt. 9:37, 38; 13:30, 39; Mark 4;29; Luke 10:2; John 4:35). In each instance, He referred to the evangelization of souls. He urged believers to pray to God, who owns the harvest, to send more laborers into His harvest so many could make it to heaven at last. Unfortunately, the enemy has continued to fight and oppose God's noble cause and purpose of salvation for humanity. He tries to engage, distract, destroy, frustrate, or otherwise employ those who should be busy on the field of souls for God.

If you are a Christian and are not winning souls or contributing to the soul-winning business, you are not wise. Be not deceived; your ministry is not doing well if soul-winning is not your primary priority.

The fruit of the righteous is a tree of life; and **he that winneth souls is wise.** *And* **they that be wise shall shine as the brightness of the firmament; and they that turn many to righteousness** *as the stars for ever and ever* (Prov. 11:30; Dan. 10:3).

This is the only work that God assigned to every Christian. We must pray for one another not to lose focus of the Great Commission.

Be ready for the final harvest

And another angel came out of the temple, crying with a loud voice to him that sat on the cloud, Thrust in thy sickle, and reap: for the time is come for thee to reap; for the harvest of the earth is ripe (Rev. 14:15).

As we approach the end of all things, it is instructive to reflect on the words of this scripture verse. Every Christian is a target. Do you know that even the earth will be harvested one day? Satan is busy destroying believers, using bitterness, unforgiveness, procrastination of restitution, competition, pride, and so forth. Do not be ignorant of his heinous devices. What will your fate be when this world is finally harvested? You must do all you can to make sure you do not disappoint God, who has planted you in the world with the hope of harvesting your soul into heaven at the end.

REFLECTIONS ON CHAPTER FOUR

The following questions may be used for personal reflections or group discussions:

1. What would you do if your season of harvest attracts criticisms and oppositions?

   _____

   _____

2. Have you figured out why some promises that God gave you have not come to pass?

   _____

   _____

3. Have you wondered why some people would rather criticize than celebrate when God has done something good in your life?

   _____

   _____

4. Which of the issues raised in this chapter relates to you, personally? How would you apply what you have learned to address these issues?

_____

_____

5. What are the indications that someone is sleeping in the ministry today?

_____

_____

6. What is your motivation for revival? Is it personal or for God's glory?

_____

_____

7. How can a church that has a great harvest opportunity increase their laborers?

_____

_____

FIVE

SENSITIVE LEADERSHP

Where Do You Stand?

And he said, be it far from me, O Lord, that I should do this: is not this the blood of the men who went in jeopardy of their lives? ***therefore he would not drink it*** (2 Sam. 23:17).

In every organization, leadership is very pivotal. Whether in the spiritual or secular, everything revolves around the leader. As noted in the life of David, he was a leader who specialized in raising ordinary men into extraordinary people; no wonder he became a general whose men got his back in challenging times. How did he earn this level of loyalty? What did these men see in him to the point of putting their lives on the line, just to quench his thirst? Why would they jeopardize their lives for the comfort of David? While these men were all committed to the God of David, it was evident that they did what they did for King David.

How many leaders still have this caliber of men in their team today? One of the many reasons why many leaders lack loyal men in their ministries today is traceable to the way they have handled the faithful and loyal men who God has mercifully brought their way. I once heard a church leader who said that he does not say "thank you" to anyone under his leadership! He felt that they were working for God. Hence, he saw no reason for any human appreciation. In his considered opinion, he believed that whatever anyone does in the church is done for God! I knew another church leader who would always ask people to help him complete specific tasks. If it was done well, he would neither acknowledge nor reply. However, if there was a mistake, he would respond promptly and demand correction. It was not long before his unappreciative attitude began to destroy the zeal of those working under him. This is one of the killers of the zeal of loyal and faithful men. On the other hand, a good leader must be able to bring his subjects out of discouragement, dejection, and feelings of unworthiness. That is what we saw in David in Adullam. When a leader is sensitive to the needs of his minions, they will always pay kind treatment back with loyal allegiance, no matter how difficult the times.

You must be determined never to be a leader who would weaken the morale of your loyal men. You must never bring them into dejection and discouragement. What are the indications of insensitive leadership? I would like to you to glean from this:

A great leader does not waste people's time

I once attended a meeting that was scheduled to last for two or three hours. Participants were asked to make contributions, and great inputs were submitted. The discussion would have ended within two hours, but the leader began to speak and continued for over two and a half hours, mostly repeating what others have already said. I have witnessed this several times, where a meeting that should last thirty minutes would continue for several hours without definite conclusions due to poor leadership coordination.

David's mighty men gave him their time, and he invested himself in them. The outcome was undeniable. Jesus did the same with His disciples. He ensured they had no regret giving Him their time and resources. If you are allowed to minister to or speak to people, do it with all the grace that God has given you. Prepare well so that the people will be grateful to God for giving such time to His cause.

Time is money, as well as life. Every second matters, and God wants you to redeem the time. When people give you their time, they commit a portion of their lives unto you, and you must ensure you help them invest it well.

A great leader does not take people's labor for granted

Be it far from me, O Lord, that I should do this (2 Sam. 23:17).

Another thing I have noticed in leadership is what I call the abuse of the power to hire and fire. This frequently happens in the one-man leadership system. A leader may soon forget those who had labored very hard with him during the difficult times. David made this mistake when he was more concerned about the life of Absalom than the lives of the people who rescued the king and the kingdom from the unforgettable rebel-led assault. It took a courageous man like Joab to call David to order. In most cases, especially when the leader is not to be questioned, such things might go unchecked and uncorrected.

I knew a man who relocated to a city and decided to join a particular church. Immediately he got there; the pastor wanted to remove the person who has been helping him with a specific task and give it to the new man. However, the new man declined the offer politely and told the pastor that he would instead develop the fellow to be more productive. The new man knew it was unfair to dump the man after he had been used to establish the church. Even God does not forget the labor of those who have faithfully served him. "For God is not unrighteous to forget your work and labor of love, which ye have shewed toward his name, in that ye have ministered to the saints, and do minister" (Heb. 6:10). If you become a leader, you must never forget those who sacrificed their comfort to hold your hands up during your weary days.

He does not fail to acknowledge those who helped him

Is not this the blood of the men who went in jeopardy of their lives? therefore he would not drink it (2 Sam. 23:17).

What are the things that would endear precious men to you? These are the things I have personally learned by experience. When your subordinates do something, don't take the glory. Don't forget to acknowledge those who played significant roles. A word of acknowledgment at the right time is more important than a thousand words of explanation after the fact.

Something the Lord Made is a 2004 American biographical movie that illustrated the partnership between the cardiac pioneer, Vivien Thomas (1910–1985), and Dr. Alfred Blalock (1899–1964), the "Blue Baby doctor" who pioneered modern heart surgery[5]. The movie narrated how Vivien Thomas, who, though was a young high school dropout, demonstrated a high level of physical skill and intellectual understanding, and confounded his boss's expectations. He swiftly became indispensable in Dr. Blalock's blue baby research program at John Hopkins. The movie illustrated that Thomas's exploits and preparations toward the first blue baby surgery brought tremendous breakthrough to the congenital heart defect problem, the Tetralogy of Fallot, also known as Blue Baby Syndrome to this day.

During this renowned world-changing project, a time came when Dr. Blalock gave a progress report and failed to invite or recognize the undeniable contributions of Vivien Thomas. Instead, Thomas watched from behind the ballroom and listened to how Blalock gave credit to the other doctors who assisted in the work but made no mention of Thomas's contributions. This scenario depicts one of the cankers that eat up the fabrics of leadership in many organizations today.

David was thoughtful and considerate in his scenario. He recognized and appreciated the sacrifice that went into bringing the water from Bethlehem. It was no easy task to break through the fierce-looking Philistines. It was a journey between life and death. They went not sure if they would return in peace or pieces. To sit and drink such water would be utter insensitivity to human sacrifice. David saw the blood of these precious men inside the jar, and not the physical water. It is wickedness to drink the sacrifice of others.

REFLECTIONS ON CHAPTER FIVE

The following questions may be used for personal reflections or group discussions:

1. How would you describe yourself— a sensitive or insensitive leader? How would people under you describe you?

i. _____

ii. _____

iii. _____

iv. _____

v. _____

2. The three men jeopardized their lives for David. Do you have a leader for whom you can do the same? Would your followers do the same or something similar for you?

3. How well do you manage peoples' time during your meetings? Rate yourself over 10.

4. Do you find it comfortable to ask for help when you are not able to perform a task?

5. When did you last ask for help from someone lower to you in rank? How did you feel about it? Do you allow people to use their gifts under your leadership?

6. Do you give credit to people for their deeds of kindness? When did you last publicly acknowledge someone who had helped you?

7. What other lessons can you learn from this chapter that could translate into improvements in your leadership style?

i. _____

ii. _____

iii. _____

iv. _____

v. _____

SIX

WHERE IS JOAB?

A Question for Church Leaders

And it came to pass, that after the year was expired, at the time that kings go out to battle, **Joab led forth the power of the army,** *and wasted the country of Ammon, and came and besieged Rabbah.* **But David tarried at Jerusalem.** *And Joab smote Rabbah, and destroyed it*
(1 Chron. 20:1).

The focus of this chapter is an uncelebrated hero—Joab. Most Bible commentaries skew the historical account of his life in favor of David. I am still wondering why most commentators have taken this path. Hence, I have decided to row against the tide and race against the wind. The Bible is not a book of honor for any man. It is God's Word to teach men the morality of God. To wrest God's Word and interpret scriptures in favor of any man would not be right.

Who was Joab?

Joab was the son of David's sister, Zeruiah, and his brothers were Abishai and Asahel. (1 Sam. 26:6). He was an intellectually razor-sharp phenomenon with unparalleled military skill, a pillar to his brethren. God used him to help his cousin, David, to get established on the most magnificent throne on earth in their time. He was a leader and mentor to his younger brothers. Countless times, he was the one that God used to rescue both the king and the entire nation. Joab became great. He was next to the king. Through his exploits, he made a name for his mother—Zeruiah, although the Bible did not say much about the life of Zeruiah, apart from the fact that she was Jesse's daughter (and Abigail's sister) and the mother of Abishai, Joab, and Asahel. Of the twenty-five verses where Zeruiah's name appears in the Bible, twenty-four were in connection with her sons. She must have been an amazing woman, whose three sons laid down their lives to preserve the anointed of the Lord and His kingdom. Joab was the commander-in-chief of the grand army of Israel. He was like a father to his two brothers, and together they rose to the highest echelon of their careers in the national army. He was a no-nonsense man, a true soldier. He and his two brothers stood with David since the time David fled from Saul, the first king of Israel.

Where is Joab? A question for church leaders

The verses in 2 Samuel 23 were the last words of David, where he recorded the exploits of his mighty men. First Chronicles 11 was a parallel passage to this. **Joab's armor-bearer** was on the list of the mighty men (2 Sam. 23:37), but Joab, whose armor he bore, was not! Abishai, his brother, was listed on both accounts. "And **Abishai, the brother of Joab,** the son of Zeruiah, was chief among three. And he lifted up his spear against three hundred, and slew them, and had the name among three" (1 Sam. 23:18; see also 1 Chron. 11:20). Even Asahel, who had died before David began to reign over the entire nation of Israel, was on both lists. "**Asahel, the brother of Joab, was one of the thirty**" (1 Sam. 23:24; 1 Chron. 11:26).

Surprisingly, in both compilations, Joab's name was missing! Why was Joab's name omitted? Many writers and Bible commentators condemned the character of Joab, especially when he disagreed with the king. However, I advise that you not jump to conclusions. Jesus told us to search the scriptures (John 5:39). God's Word has no favorite, and I hope each leader in the body of Christ would find time to reflect on the issues raised in this book.

I know you might have a sentiment for David. Many commentators do as well. However, I do not believe that the Bible is written to give preference to anyone. God's Word is inspired so we could learn all that God has for us therein. The issues before us are crucial and profound. Where is Joab? Why did David remove his name from the list of his mighty men? Please join me to analyze the five scenarios where Joab disagreed with David. I believe God will shed some light on your heart as you glean through.

Scenario 1—The issue of numbering Israel

And again the anger of the LORD *was kindled against Israel, and he moved David against them to say, Go, number Israel and Judah. For the king said to Joab the captain of the host, which was with him, Go now through all the tribes of Israel, from Dan even to Beersheba, and number ye the people, that I may know the number of the people. And Joab said unto the king, Now the* LORD *thy God add unto the people, how many soever they be, an hundredfold, and that the eyes of my lord the king may see it: but why doth my lord the king delight in this thing? Notwithstanding the king's word prevailed against Joab, and against the captains of the host. And Joab and the captains of the host went out from the presence of the king, to number the people of Israel* (2 Sam. 24:2–4).

In 1 Chronicles 21:1, it was noted that David was under satanic manipulation at this point in his life. Therefore, it is clear that David's spiritual life was not okay at this time. Second Samuel 24:1 says David had even lost God's favor at this time. He was spiritually dead. To the contrary, Joab was spiritually sensitive and mindful of the God of Israel. He even performed the role of a prophet to David when no seer was around. Joab already foresaw that David's action would displease God (1 Chron. 21:3–7). He knew danger was imminent. Hence, I believe Joab was an honest and God-fearing man. He was no hypocrite, unlike many Christian workers who would never tell their leaders the truth. Joab was not so. He politely queried David's motive. *And Joab said unto the king, Now the* LORD *thy God add unto the people, how many soever they be, an hundredfold, and that the eyes of my lord the king may see it:* **but why doth my lord the king delight in this thing?** (2 Sam. 24:3).

Perhaps, David was offended at Joab's correction. Many leaders do not appreciate anyone questioning their authority. Eventually, the census took Joab and his team nine months and twenty days! If any of their wives were to be pregnant at the time they left, she would have delivered the baby before they returned! It was a colossal waste of almost a year. *So when they had gone through all the land, they came to Jerusalem at the end of* **nine months and twenty days** (2 Sam. 24:8).

Think of the resources and the number of Christian workers who were committedly doing a work that God did not send the church. It is sad to note that many of today's church leaders are only wasting the lives, potentials, and destinies of their followers and workers on non-essential church traditions. In several denominations, people are investing hours and years teaching for doctrines the commandments of a man at the terrifying expense of God's Word.

Conceivably, if Joab had insisted, some folks around the king would have called him a rebel. However, David's action had caused the untimely death of seventy thousand Israelites before his eyes were opened! Calamity had begun before David repented, and before God's Word went to Prophet Gad. It took the mercy of God over Jerusalem for Him to stop the plague that would have wiped out the capital city of Israel. Had the king listened to the words of Joab, those innocent lives would have been preserved. Moreover, such a waste of time and other resources would have been avoided if leadership opinion had not prevailed over the helpless voice of truth.

In the end, there was no indication that Joab mocked David when it became evident that the king's action had resulted in severe trouble for the entire nation. Also, there was no record that David apologized to Joab, who had earlier advised against the king's action. I see this as the primary problem of most one-man leadership systems, where a church leader has nobody to question him/her. That is a dangerous position to be in as a leader. A leader who is not answerable to any man must be very careful with such an office. As a leader, it is not compulsory that you must have the final word in every meeting. God might be pleased to lend His wisdom through some of your subordinates. Sometimes God could even use a child to advise the parent. Unfortunately, many leaders only listen to counter whatever anyone under them has to say. A leader who does not listen is a potential danger to himself and those under him. Do not be a leader who cannot be advised.

In this matter, I believe Joab deserved commendation. Sadly, he would have to be punished for speaking the truth.

Scenario 2—The issue of Abner's death

Abner was the captain of Saul's army. Immediately after Saul's death, Abner made himself strong for Saul's house (2 Sam. 3:6), making Ishbosheth the king. Abner did not hand over the kingdom to David, even though he knew that God had given David the kingdom (2 Sam. 3:9). This confirmed that Abner was not a righteous man. He worked tirelessly against the purpose of God. Only the tribe of Judah accepted David as their king (2 Sam. 2:11). During this time, Abner repeatedly came to challenge the army of David to battle. Joab led David's army against the Abner-led army of Saul, and Joab's team always defeated Abner's team.

"Now there was long war between the house of Saul and the house of David: but David waxed stronger and stronger, and the house of Saul waxed weaker and weaker" (2 Sam. 3:1).

However, in one of those wars, Abner killed Joab's brother, Asahel. In an attempt to revenge their brother's death, Joab and Abishai pursued Abner until Abner diplomatically surrendered (2 Sam. 2:26,27). Abner's defeat was palpable, but he pleaded with Joab to end the war so that more people would not die. Joab therefore told his army to retreat from destroying Abner's army (2 Sam. 2:28–31).

Joab was a good man to have ended the war for the sake of the innocent lives. However, Abner went to David without Joab's knowledge and presented himself to David. While Joab and the other soldiers went to bury Asahel, Abner had quickly gone to have a private meeting with David in the palace. He knew the battle was sore against him as his defeat was imminent. Hence,

Abner acted mischievously. He pretended as if his motives were of God, but that move was dubious.

In addition to Abner's defeat, Ishbosheth refused to let him have his father's concubine.

> *And Saul had a concubine, whose name was Rizpah, the daughter of Aiah: and Ishbosheth said to Abner, Wherefore hast thou gone in unto my father's concubine? Then was Abner very wroth for the words of Ishbosheth, and said, Am I a dog's head, which against Judah do shew kindness this day unto the house of Saul thy father, to his brethren, and to his friends, and have not delivered thee into the hand of David, that thou chargest me to day with a fault concerning this woman? So do God to Abner, and more also, except, as the LORD hath sworn to David, even so I do to him; To translate the kingdom from the house of Saul, and to set up the throne of David over Israel and over Judah, from Dan even to Beersheba* (2 Sam. 3:7–10).

It is evident from the above scripture that Abner's reason for wanting to hand over the remaining tribes to David was due to the misunderstanding he had with Ishbosheth and the defeat he had just suffered in the hands of Joab.

Noteworthily, Abner did not tell David that Joab defeated him in the battle. He came to David as if he was a champion. Abner negotiated an alliance with David, knowing that his defeat and loss of the kingdom was looming. He secretly asked David to make a league with him. Scripture was silent about what the league between David and Abner entailed. However, Abner would likely have a prominent office in the United Kingdom of Israel.

This scenario further revealed several other omissions in David's life. The goal here is not to water down David's integrity during the low moments of his life. Rather, the goal is to shine the torchlight of scriptures on this dark side of the king's life, as they are not worthy of emulation for the New Testament saints.

Let us consider some of David's lapses in this matter as revealed in scriptures:

One, while Abner came to negotiate the kingdom with David, David was more concerned about the wife that Saul gave him. The issue of women seems to be a weakness in David's life. Recall the terrible risk he took to get the dowry for Michal, Saul's daughter, showed that he could do anything when it comes to women's issues (1 Sam. 18:25–27). The matter of Bathsheba also attested to this. He married Bathsheba immediately after Uriah died. Again, the way he quickly married Abigail after Nabal's death raised some moral questions for the thinking Christian.

Two, David mourned for Abner. Many Bible scholars have written that David was kind to have wept over the death of Abner. However, I have a different opinion about this. Jesus said, **"Love your enemy," but He did not say hate your friends.** David's action here is questionable. His reaction in this situation is not consistent with God's principles of morality, fairness, and justice. The New Testament saint must be wary of this kind of attitude. Sometimes leaders could be carried away with projects at the expense of the people over which God had made them overseers. Come to think of it, Abner had been a longstanding enemy of David. He did not tell David that he had killed one of his choice soldiers. Remember that Asahel was the son of David's sister, Zeruiah. He was also the brother of Joab, who was David's right-hand man. Asahel died in a battle to preserve David as king. If David were to be fair, he should have mourned for Asahel, too, his sister's son.

Was it not surprising that David mourned for Abner, but there was no record that David shed a tear for Asahel, one of his mighty men who was recently killed by Abner?

Perhaps, David mourned Abner's death to remove suspicion from him and show that he had no hand in Abner's death (2 Sam. 3:28). It was also an opportunity for David to gain the favor of all the tribes. Such an act would pave the way for his reign over the other tribes who had been under Abner.

Three, Joab had just lost a brother and a mighty man in the army. He and the other soldiers had just gone from that same war where Abner and his team were defeated to bury Asahel, whom Abner had killed. Joab and the other soldiers had not even returned from the battle. In a brief meeting, David had agreed with Abner without consulting with Joab and his army. It was quite shocking that David already entered into a league with Abner, the enemy. Again, David seemed to have relaxed in his spiritual sensitivity.

Joab had just lost his dear brother in battle. Coming home, he found out that David had given his position to Abner. Whereas Joab was the one who had been fighting for the house of David, while Abner defended the house of Saul. *And it came to pass, while there was **war between the house of Saul and the house of David**, that **Abner made himself strong for the house of Saul*** (2 Sam. 3:6).

If Abner was not condemned for killing Asahel, why condemn Joab for killing Abner? As a warrior, he had his reasons for killing Abner. One, in revenge for his slain brother, which is acceptable in warfare (2 Sam. 3:30). Two, to protect David from a likely evil in the hands of Abner. Three, to preserve his own life because it was impossible to have two commanders-in-chief in the same army. I wondered why David was not happy with Joab in this matter. Perhaps, there could be more to this than the death of wily Abner.

Scenario 3—The issue of Absalom

Absalom was known for his unbridled rebellion. Everyone, including David, knew he was a terrible fellow. He killed Amnon, his brother, as a revenge for raping his sister (2 Sam. 13:28–34). When David and Absalom could not see face to face, it was this same Joab who saw the need to reconcile them (2 Sam. 14). After Absalom's restoration, he plotted a coup that sent his father on exile, and he took over the government. Ahithophel, who was David's advisor and the entire tribe of Judah, also defected with him. Absalom slept with David's concubine in public (2 Sam 16:21, 22) and made himself king. He also appointed his cousin, Amasa, as captain of the army as a replacement for Joab. The entire nation was in turmoil. It was Joab that God used to rescue David, his wives, and all his other children.

Despite Absalom's evil deed, David remained biased. He cherished his ruthless, murderous, ungodly, self-conceited, and rebellious son more than his loyal and faithful soldiers. Both Joab and David were on Absalom's death row. Absalom's act was a felony. Though David had asked Joab and Abishai to deal gently with Absalom, it was evident that David's request at this time was selfish. Joab put his life on the line and killed Absalom to preserve David's life and that of many other innocent lives (2 Sam. 18).

> *And it was told Joab, Behold, the king weepeth and mourneth for Absalom. And the victory that day was turned into mourning unto all the people: for the people heard say that day how the king was grieved for his son. And the people gat them by stealth that day into the city, as people being ashamed steal away when they flee in battle. But the king covered his face, and the king cried with a*

loud voice, O my son Absalom, O Absalom, my son, my son! And Joab came into the house to the king, and said, Thou hast shamed this day the faces of all thy servants, which this day have saved thy life, and the lives of thy sons and of thy daughters, and the lives of thy wives, and the lives of thy concubines; In that thou lovest thine enemies, and hatest thy friends. For thou hast declared this day, that thou regardest neither princes nor servants: for this day I perceive, that if Absalom had lived, and all we had died this day, then it had pleased thee well. Now therefore arise, go forth, and speak comfortably unto thy servants: for I swear by the LORD, if thou go not forth, there will not tarry one with thee this night: and that will be worse unto thee than all the evil that befell thee from thy youth until now. Then the king arose, and sat in the gate. And they told unto all the people, saying, Behold, the king doth sit in the gate. And all the people came before the king: for Israel had fled every man to his tent (2 Sam 19:1–7).

Again, David's action was questionable here, but no one could tell the anointed of the Lord as no one was ready to bell the cat. However, someone needed to help the king do the right thing. At some point in life, every leader might need someone to help him do the right. In our time, many leaders have gone so low to act like David in this regard.

Many church systems are rotting away because everybody is afraid to tell the leader the truth. Joab was that man who would always tell the truth as it is. Such men are rare today, who will stand to say to the "Peter" in the church that *...he was to be blamed* (Gal. 2:11).

Joab found himself between a rock and a hard place. He was faced with a difficult choice—to choose between a failing father and a wicked son. However, rather than compromise his integrity, Joab decided to please God. He would neither please a compromising leader nor follow an unruly one.

David's reaction put to shame all the people who had endangered their lives for him (2 Sam. 19:1–4). It was very disappointing to his faithful subjects to find David mourning for the very enemy they battled to destroy so that he and his household and kingdom might live. Joab had to save the day for David. He censured David but gave him more sensible advice (2 Sam. 19:5–7). David had no choice but to obey the righteous request of Joab (2 Sam. 19:5). David arose and went to the right place he should have been—the gate (2 Sam. 19:8). But rather than appreciate Joab, he decided to punish him!

Following Joab's correction of David on the matter of his mourning for Absalom, David told everybody that he had handed over Joab to God (2 Sam. 3:39) but secretly told Solomon to kill Joab (1 Kings 2:5)!

Following Absalom's death and Joab's correction, David's next action was to bribe the tribe of Judah by offering to give their candidate—Amasa—a key position in the kingdom (2 Sam 19:11–15). David played tribal politics. He wanted his tribe to be the first to welcome him, and he knew the only person who could hinder the tribe of Judah from accepting his invitation was Amasa, who Absalom had appointed. David's tribal sentiments also created jealousy and a division of the kingdom God had already won for him (2 Sam. 19:41—20:1–2). Unfortunately, tribalism and politics have also gained traction in the church today.

David must have felt that Joab had become too strong for him to manipulate. Therefore, he planned to replace a righteous Joab, who had been the most loyal person to him, with a traitor,

Amasa, who had just led a brutal revolt against his empire alongside his unruly son—Absalom (2 Sam. 19:13). We see this played out in churches today, where a leader believes he has the absolute power to hire and fire anyone in the church. Anyone who crosses the leader's path must be punished or removed, even when the leader is obviously at fault.

In another scenario, Joab's brother, Abishai, suggested to David that Shimei, who had earlier cursed the anointed of the Lord, should die, but David scathingly rebuked him.

> *But Abishai the son of Zeruiah answered and said, Shall not Shimei be put to death for this, because he cursed the LORD's anointed?* **And David said, What have I to do with you, ye sons of Zeruiah, that ye should this day be adversaries unto me? Shall there any man be put to death this day in Israel? for do not I know that I am this day king over Israel?** (2 Sam. 19:21, 22).

By David's reaction, it was evident that he was angry with both Joab and Abishai. Even though it was Abishai who spoke, David, in his response, addressed both Abishai, Joab, and their mother when he said, "ye sons of Zeruiah." David pretended before the people as if Abishai's suggestion was terrible, whereas he had determined a worse plan against Shimei. Indeed, the heart of man is desperately wicked (Jer. 17:9). David even swore to Shimei that he would not kill him (2 Sam. 19:23) but secretly mandated Solomon to ensure Shimei was murdered (1 Kings 2:8, 9)! People might call this an act of diplomacy today, but I believe Jesus would call it hypocrisy. Jesus would not mince words about it. O, how we must pray for our leaders as this is becoming common in the church today.

Scenario 4—The issue of Amasa

Amasa was also a debased fellow like Absalom, who conspired with Absalom against David and Joab. They were birds of a feather. During the apparent overthrow, Absalom appointed Amasa to replace Joab. What an insult to the king and Joab! There is no question about whether Amasa should die. In the face of reality, his offense was punishable by death. Even though the battle had stopped, there was no indication that Amasa had repented. Amasa's headiness was evident in the fact that he and the entire tribe of Judah did not accept David as their king, even though their self-appointed rebellious king, Absalom, had died (2 Sam. 19:9, 10). Had Joab not killed Amasa, both David and Solomon might have eventually died like fools. It was strange again that David would ask Solomon to punish Joab for another act of faithfulness that Joab demonstrated toward him and his house. Many leaders in the church make similar mistakes today. They make wrong decisions just because they did not want to agree with a subordinate person. On what moral basis would David replace Joab with Amasa? Why did David pretend as if he had forgiven Shimei when he had a different motive in his heart? These are not traits to be emulated by the New Testament Christians.

Scenario 5—The matter of Adonijah

At the time when Adonijah declared himself king over Israel, David's reaction during Absalom's rebellion might have confused Joab. Since Adonijah was Absalom's brother from the same mother, Joab might have decided to support Adonijah, thinking David would be wrath with him AGAIN if he did otherwise. *Then tidings came to Joab: for Joab had turned after Adonijah, **though he turned not after Absalom*** (1 Kgs. 2:28).

David had not told Joab that Solomon would be his successor. According to 1 Kings 1:11–18, it appeared to have been a secret between David, Bathsheba, Solomon, and Nathan. "*And she said unto him, My lord, thou* **swarest by the Lord thy God unto thine handmaid, saying, Assuredly Solomon thy son shall reign after me, and he shall sit upon my throne.** *And now, behold, Adonijah reigneth; and now, my lord the king, thou knowest it not*" (1 Kgs. 1:17, 18).

We were not told in Scripture why and when David promised Bathsheba that he would make her son succeed him on the throne. However, it is believable that Prophet Nathan must have been in the full picture. He was the prophet that God sent to minister unto David in the matter of Uriah, and it was Prophet Nathan who instructed Bathsheba to go in and remind David of the agreement between him and Bathsheba.

Nathan spoke to Bathsheba, the mother of Solomon, saying: *Go and get thee in unto king David, and say unto him,* **Didst not thou, my lord, O king, swear unto thine handmaid, saying, Assuredly Solomon thy son shall reign after me, and he shall sit upon my throne?** *why then doth Adonijah reign?* (1 Kgs. 1:13).

It was interesting to note that David only revealed this prophetic secret to Solomon toward the end of his life. Probably, this top-secret eventually leaked into the ears of Adonijah.

> *And David said, Solomon my son is young and tender, and the house that is to be builded for the Lord must be exceeding magnifical, of fame and of glory throughout all countries: I will therefore now make preparation for it. So David prepared abundantly before his death. Then he called for Solomon his son, and charged him to build an house for the Lord God of Israel. And David said*

*to Solomon, My son, as for me, it was in my mind to build an house unto the name of the Lord my God: But the word of the Lord came to me, saying, Thou hast shed blood abundantly, and hast made great wars: thou shalt not build an house unto my name, because thou hast shed much blood upon the earth in my sight. **Behold, a son shall be born to thee**, who shall be a man of rest; and I will give him rest from all his enemies round about: **for his name shall be Solomon**, and I will give peace and quietness unto Israel in his days* (1 Chron. 22:5–9)

From the above Scripture, it was clear that God told David that a son, born to him, whose name would be Solomon, would be king after him. The name "Solomon" was one of the seven names in the Bible, given by God before the child was born. Before Solomon's birth, God already gave the prophecy that David's successor be named Solomon because Solomon means rest. God promised to give rest to Israel during his reign. However, it was not clear if God ever told David which of his wives would give birth to that specific son. We are unsure whether God instructed David that the son to be named Solomon would be from Bathsheba, or David took that decision out of his own volition. Interestingly, when Solomon was born, David called him Solomon, but God sent Nathan to name him Jedidiah *because of the Lord* (2 Sam. 12:24,25).

Could this be a reward orchestrated by God in honor of Uriah? Was it the token of restitution to Bathsheba for dishonoring her purity and for the death of her loving and faithful husband? Only eternity would reveal this to us.

In all of Bible records, it was only in the matter of Adonijah that Joab did not support David. Even when David was not sincere or supportive of his own life, Joab had always stood to defend him. Having loved David, he loved him until the end.

As noted under the issue of Absalom above, David's reaction must have put Joab in an awkward position as David never checked Absalom. When Joab acted in David's favor against Absalom, David was not happy with him. Even when Absalom took power into his hands and killed Amnon, David said nothing. The unchecked indiscipline of Absalom by the king might have also given Adonijah an impression that if he too could overthrow the kingdom, perhaps his father would never mind. Notably, David had never challenged whatever Adonijah did.

Then Adonijah the son of Haggith exalted himself, saying, I will be king: and he prepared him chariots and horsemen, and fifty men to run before him. **And his father had not displeased him at any time in saying, why hast thou done so?** *and he also was a very goodly man; and his mother bare him after Absalom* (1 Kgs. 1:5, 6).

Considering that Adonijah, who was brother to Absalom, had decided to do the same thing, naturally, Joab might have followed him, based on David's reaction during Absalom's revolt. Moreover, David was old at this time.

And he (Adonijah) conferred with Joab the son of Zeruiah, and with Abiathar the priest: and they following Adonijah helped him (1 Kings 1:7).

Recall that David was angry with Joab for opposing and killing Absalom, and he did not hide it. Adonijah might have thought that since he was next to Absalom, perhaps he was the heir to the throne. "Then the king was deeply moved, and went up to the chamber over the gate, and wept. And as he went, he said thus: "O my son Absalom—my son, my son Absalom—if only I had died in your place! O Absalom my son, my son!" (2 Sam. 18:33).

According to the Scripture, the decision to take over the throne was Adonijah's, not Joab's.

And he (Adonijah) said, **Thou knowest that the kingdom was mine**, *and that all Israel set their faces on me, that I should reign: howbeit the kingdom is turned about, and is become my brother's: for it was his from the Lord* (1 Kgs. 2:15).

Perhaps Joab might have learned by experience to play along with the wishes of the king's kids by compromising his integrity to please a leader whose morality had become questionable based on scriptures. Nevertheless, since Joab knew that which was right, he should have refused to compromise.

Why should Joab die?

After the death of Absalom, Sheba, the son of Bichri, led another coup plot against David and his kingdom. At this time, David bypassed Joab and asked Abishai to lead the team and assigned Amasa to gather the tribe of Judah. However, had it not been for Joab's timely intervention, it would have been a disaster for David and his house again. Even though David had replaced Joab at this time, yet, Joab still went after David's enemy. As Joab and his men were pursuing David's new rival, Sheba, they met Amasa, by the way, who had already put on Joab's official uniform! Joab must have been so shocked to see Amasa wearing his official uniform. By implication, Joab's life was no longer safe. Since it was impossible to have two ministers of defense in the same army, Joab had to play smart. He killed Amasa.

> *And Amasa wallowed in blood in the midst of the highway. And when the man saw that all the people stood still, he removed Amasa out of the highway into the field, and cast a cloth upon*

*him, when he saw that every one that came by him stood still. When he was removed out of the highway, **all the people went on after Joab, to pursue after Sheba, the son of Bichri** (2 Sam. 20:12, 13).*

Joab did not mind David's ingratitude and disloyalty to him. He and his men continued until they saw the end of David's enemy, and Joab and his team returned to David with the head of Sheba, as a token of their victory (2 Sam. 20:14–22). It was Joab again that saved the situation. Let me ask again, what was Joab's sin in all of these?

It was appalling that in the end, David still charged Solomon to avenge the death of both Abner and Amasa on Joab. To convince Solomon, he said both men (Abner and Amasa) were better than Joab. If they were better, why did they not defeat Joab all these years? If what David said was true, why did Joab always defeat Abner in all the wars they fought, even though Abner had more soldiers on his side? If Amasa was better than Joab, then Absalom would have reigned.

Many leaders in the church act like David in these dramatic scenarios. They discipline anyone who challenges or disagrees with them on any issue. To disagree with a leader on a moral ground is not sinful, even as it is evident that God did not approve of David's conduct in all these matters. Joab was loyal to the God of David but disagreed with David on administrative issues.

After rescuing David's life and that of his family, including Solomon, it was not fair to reward him with such heinous punitive measures.

Notably, Joab understood spiritual things. He could discern when death was imminent, even before Solomon gave the order for his execution. When death was near, Joab refused to die a fool. Instead of defending himself, he committed his life to Jehovah's hands. He handed over to God what he could no longer protect—his life, to gain what he would never lose—eternal life.

And Joab fled unto the tabernacle of the Lord, and caught hold on the horns of the altar (1 Kgs. 2:28).

To Joab, there was no better place to end his race than at the feet of His Lord. Jesus is the horn of salvation for every man. Joab placed himself on the altar as a living sacrifice. He knew the horn of the altar was the place of forgiveness and mercy, and that was enough for him in the face of death. Joab died *a scapegoat and was sent into eternal wilderness* by the hands of one of the men he once trained and mentored! In his case, *it was he that dippeth his hand with him in the dish that betrayed him* (Matt. 26:23). Even though Benaiah knew it was wrong to slay a man who had gone to lay hold of the horn of the altar, he had no choice but to comply with the unquestionable king's rule.

Ironically, Joab was the only soldier in David's army, who was officially slain by a fellow squad member. Though earlier, under David's instruction, Joab was instructed to retreat from Uriah to let him die, it was not Joab that killed Uriah. It was David who killed Uriah, and the scripture is clear about it. God told David, "Wherefore hast thou despised the commandment of the Lord, to do evil in his sight? Thou hast killed Uriah the Hittite with the sword, and hast taken his wife to be thy wife, **and hast slain him with the sword of the children of Ammon**" (2 Sam. 12:9). Also, from the study of scriptures and comparisons of events during that time, I believe this was the point when David began to lose reputation in Joab's eyes. When Joab discovered what David had done, his reaction showed that he did not like it. It is obvious how he related with David in subsequent battles when David stayed back at home (2 Sam. 12:27–31). David's counselor, Ahithophel, who was Bathsheba's grandfather, must have also lost confidence in David's leadership because of David's dastardly act. That could be Ahithophel's primary reason for decamping to Absalom, to dethrone David.

Uriah's murder was the sin that gave birth to the other sins in King David's life. It was one sin too many as it was written that David obeyed all that God commanded him all the days of his life, with an exception because of what he did to Uriah (1 Kgs. 15:5).

On the other hand, Solomon knew the importance of holding on to the horn of the altar. Everybody knew the horn of the altar was the place of forgiveness and mercy. Solomon forgave sinful and rebellious Adonijah when he fled to hold on to the horns of the altar (1 Kings 1:50-53). However, when Joab, who had never sinned against Solomon, held on to the horns of the altar, he told Benaiah to kill him there! We must always remember that Solomon only killed Adonijah when he touched the untouchable side of his life—women.

Did not Solomon king of Israel sin by these things? Yet among many nations was there no king like him, who was beloved of his God, and God made him king over all Israel: nevertheless even him did outlandish women cause to sin (Neh. 13:26).

It was evident that moral weakness on the issue of women was a problem in David's household. Amnon died for this same evil. Absalom slept with his father's concubine and hastened himself to an untimely death. Adonijah died because he could not overcome his lust for the fair damsel, Abishag.

It was a deficiency in David's life. Hence, he had no moral strength to correct it in the lives of his children. A man can only correct a sin that he has overcome (2 Cor. 10:6). Jesus pointed the attention of his disciples to this when he said, *How wilt thou say to thy brother, let me pull out the mote out of thine eye; and, behold, a beam is in thine own eye? Thou hypocrite, first cast out* the beam out of thine own eye; and then shalt thou see clearly to cast out the mote out of thy brother's eye (Matt. 7:4,5).

No doubt, David started well. He pleased God well, becoming the apple of God's eyes as a humble shepherd boy, and he attained an honorary degree before the heaven and the earth. He stood before the king, and it was notable in scriptures that he served God in his generation (Acts 13:36).

An important question to ask is, why did David not tell Solomon to kill Adonijah, who was the actual culprit? Why was David silent on Abiathar, considering he was also part of the coup? It was surprising to hear Solomon said he showed mercy to Abiathar because he stood with his father in all his troubles. Whereas were it not for Joab, both Solomon and his mother would have been long dead by Abner's wicked attempts, and the evil conspiracies of Absalom, Amasa, and Sheba. It appeared David's sense of morality declined as his power increased. He seemed to have *built again the thing which he had earlier destroyed during his youthful years* (Gal. 2:18).

Many people started with a high sense of morality and justice. However, as they gained position and fame, they seemed to begin to overlook the weightier matters of God's law (Matt. 23:23). It was disconcerting to note by the way David killed Uriah and the speed with which Bathsheba became his wife at a time when the king should have been fighting for the glory of the Lord (2 Sam. 11). David mourned for Saul before he became king. However, after David became king, no tear was shed for the death of his own friends—Uriah and Asahel. When David was younger, he would never avenge himself, not even against Saul, who made several attempts to kill him. But in old age, David could avenge himself on Joab because Joab had challenged his authority on sensitive administrative issues. David told Shimei he had forgiven him. David even swore that Shimei would not die. Yet, he secretly asked Solomon to kill him! Is this not the condition of many leaders today?

> And, behold, thou hast with thee Shimei the son of Gera, a Benjamite of Bahurim, which cursed me with a grievous curse in the day when I went to Mahanaim: **but he came down to meet me at Jordan, and I sware to him by the LORD, saying, I will not put thee to death with the sword. Now therefore hold him not guiltless:** for thou art a wise man, and knowest what thou oughtest to do unto him; **but his hoar head bring thou down to the grave with blood** (1 Kgs. 2:8, 9).

Frightening to mention that the last word from the mouth of David was blood. Many leaders today are guilty of this as well. They pretend to be holy and act as if they are not offended, but inwardly, they would seek occasion to punish someone who had crossed their path. Even when an apology has been rendered, and they said, "No problem," only a discerning mind would know that it is not yet over. They would always seek an opportunity for reprisal. Lord Acton said, "Power corrupts, and that absolute power corrupts absolutely." I believe this is an issue for all leaders to reflect upon.

David's last and revengeful words about Joab seems to be laden with some unconfessed malice. Unfortunately, it is a general assumption that if a person disagrees with a leader, he must be wrong. Severally, church folks usually consider such people to be sinners or backsliders, without checking the facts of the matter. In the church today, it appears the leader must always be right. Many people "disciplined" by leaders are already condemned by everybody before the truth usually comes out. In most instances, the leaders do not ever get to make their restitution to the offended people, and God may not be well pleased. This canker limits God's presence in the body of Christ.

According to 2 Samuel 23, the reflection on David's mighty men was his last poem. Hence, David must have removed Joab's name because of the disagreements Joab had with him on the pertinent issues I raised above. Could this be an untold omission in the life of David? The fact that David instructed Solomon to kill Joab and Shimei confirmed that David did not forgive before he died, even though it is debatable to say if Joab had sinned against him or God.

In my opinion, the New Testament believer should not stand to defend the Old Testament saints when their lives fall short of Christ's standard. Embedded within David's last words were unspoken motives of revenge and unforgiveness, which fall below Christ's standard for the New Testament saints. *For if ye forgive men their trespasses, your heavenly Father will also forgive you: But if ye forgive not men their trespasses, neither will your Father forgive your trespasses* (Matt. 6:14,15). During David's transition hours, he gave the characteristics of an ideal leader— "He that ruleth over men must be just, ruling in the fear of God" (2 Sam. 23:3), but his action depicted otherwise!

How many leaders today preach what is not real in their lives. As a follower of Christ, we must let our doing precede our preaching and teachings. Luke told us, "of all that Jesus began both to **do and teach**" (Acts 1:1). That is the standard of Christ for His church. Church leaders must beware of these destructive tendencies. The latent omissions of leadership that were apparent in David's life call for solemn self-examination. These are unspoken truths as it appears that David's beginning was more glorious than his latter days. If these things happened to the "apple of God's eyes, it behooves everyone leading in one capacity or the other today to reflect circumspectly. Beware of using your position, power, and authority to punish the helpless but righteous people who are endeavoring to tell you the truth. Do not think yourself to be right all the time.

Notably, there was no indication that any of the curses that David placed upon Joab were fulfilled anywhere in the Scriptures. All the post-exilic families, whose ancestries were named Joab happened to be noblemen (Ezra 2:6; 8:9; Neh. 7:11), although these may not be related to Joab, the son of Zeruiah.

Maliciously, Solomon was instructed to kill perhaps, the only voice that might have warned him from going astray and possibly prevent the disintegration of the ten tribes from the house of David, and he did! This is how many church leaders unknowingly destroy the person that God sent to them to fulfill the purpose of God in their ministry. Solomon killed Joab and became a king who could not be questioned by anyone and did whatever he liked, but the consequences were grave.

Based on David's charge to Solomon, Abner and Amasa's deaths were the "sins" of Joab, but in all fairness, none of David's claims warranted a penalty of death for Joab. Permit me to ask, if Joab was David's son, would David ask Solomon to avenge Abner and Amasa's death on him? Why did David not punish Absalom when he murdered his brother – Amnon? Why was David so sad when Absalom died but showed no concern for Asahel and Uriah? Why did David not ask Solomon to avenge on Adonijah for his insurrection?

Many commentators might call Joab a murderer and David a saint. However, if Joab deserved to die, then David would have deserved to die many more times. Considering the situation at that dispensation, both Abner and Amasa deserved to die. David only played tribal politics and a superiority complex with the throne, and the scripture was not silent about these facts (2 Sam. 19:11–14).

Like Joab, if you find yourself under a bad leader, you don't have to continue with him and cause problems for yourself.

Conflicts and contention in the church might eventually cause you an eternal loss. If your leader refuses to change or do God's will, you must pray and be sure that God would want you to continue with him. Otherwise, it would be better not to be involved than to be involved but 'disobedient' or 'unruly.'

For example, in the matter of numbering Israel, Joab knew it was wrong. Nevertheless, he went for the assignment and counted only ten but not the entire twelve tribes. According to the Scriptures, Joab did not count Levi and Benjamin because *the king's word was abominable* (1 Chron. 21:6). Perhaps, it would have been better for Joab to have left David when the king's instruction was contrary to God's will or after Uriah's death. That way, Joab would have gone away from the leadership stage without any blemish to his integrity. Just as Uriah's faithfulness did, Joab's insistence on that which was right might have as well brought to light another dark side of David's leadership. Such were men like John the Baptist. He would neither be involved nor remain silent over the king's sin (Mark 6:17,18). He stood for the truth and went to the prison to die, and to rest in peace. Although such men may be considered foolish by men, God holds them in high esteem (John 12:26).

Moreover, it would have been more honorable for Joab to leave the king and his children to play their game, rather than allow himself to be confused or compromised with another spoilt child, like Absalom.

Joab, which means **Jehovah is Father**, lived true to his name. He gave all he had to defend Jehovah's cause under David. Wherever duty or danger called, Joab was always there for the king. He had fought for the right cause all his life.

Had Joab insisted on that which was right during Adonijah's time, as he did during Absalom's rebellion, he might have ended well. It would have been quite difficult for David to appeal to Solomon's emotion to kill him. However, David knew that

Solomon would easily associate Joab with Adonijah's sins, since Adonijah had earlier attempted to steal the throne from him.

Where is the Joab in your church today? How are you rewarding your Joab? How did you handle those who have faithfully served God under you but disagreed with you on administrative issues? Perhaps, you have already killed your own Joab, like Solomon. May God shine His light on your heart before it is too late. I pray you would not be too busy with the temple building and not find time to repent. To all the "Joabs" going through similar experiences today, I encourage you to stay on course for God alone. Stand for that which is right, but avoid the errors and mistakes of Zeruiah's eldest son.

May God help us all.

REFLECTIONS ON CHAPTER SIX

The following questions may be used for personal reflections or group discussions:

1. Can you think of a woman like Zeruiah in your church, whose kids are all faithfully serving the purpose of God? How have you rewarded them? List the ones you know or remember.

   i. _____

   ii. _____

   iii. _____

2. Can you think of a man like Joab in your church, who brings young people to church or encouraged younger people to get involved in the work of the ministry? How are you treating such folks? List the ones you know or remember and answer the questions above.

   i. _____

   ii. _____

   iii. _____

iv. _____

v. _____

3. As a leader, have you ever been involved in a situation where someone corrected you, but you refused to listen, only to realize later that you were wrong? What did you do? Did you think you should make any restitution in this regard?

_____

_____

4. How do you feel when someone lower than you have some spiritual gifts that you do not have?

_____

_____

5. Do you appreciate someone who sincerely or constructively criticizes or questions your motives?

_____

_____

6. Which should be more important to the leader—The people he is leading or the kingdom projects to be urgently executed?

_____

_____

7. Should a leader always have the final word on every matter? Give reasons for your answer

_____

_____

SEVEN

DAVID AND HIS MIGHTY MEN

Sundry Lessons for All

And when David heard of it, he sent Joab, and all the host of the mighty men (2 Sam. 10:7; 1 Chron. 19:8).

As considered in this book, David and his mighty men's lives presents several questions and lessons to every believer. To wrap it up, let us attempt to look at *seven* specific issues that God might still want us to press further and pray about.

One, it was a noteworthy fact that most of the men who made up the army of Israel during David's reign were aliens! What happened to the Israelites who should have been at the forefront of the battle of the Lord? As I read through these men's transition period, my mind went to the church, where I received most of my spiritual training. I noticed that majority of the workers were not born into the church. Most of the spiritually vital folks came into the church as they were seeking a "cave of Adullam" where the gifts of God in their lives would be stirred up. I could remember how we used to sometimes meet for prayers in our hideouts and pray for numerous hours. Occasionally, we met over days, and often we tarried before God for innumerable hours. I once stayed somewhere where we had to meet for fellowship in the bush because of the enemies.

Today, one cannot but ask, what is wrong with this generation? This is the question emanating from my personal experience in the church. In those days, it was compulsory to go through about one-year practical and goal-oriented training before you could do anything in the church. Today, the church has grown. However, I saw that leadership focus has shifted from Workers' Prayer Meetings to Workers' Planning Meetings. Leaders and workers could hold planning meetings for a whole day, without a concerted one-hour prayer, and sometimes, a weeklong meeting without one day of fasting and prayers! Everything is now centered on planning and organizing. In the past, leaders agonized, and we saw the glory. Today, leaders could even organize how and when the Holy Ghost would be involved in church programs! Organizers, orators, and clowns had suddenly outnumbered the agonizers in church leadership. In several places, everything has become cold and dry, while in some others, everything appears lively except for the evident absence of the divine. The people are happy but unrepentant.

In many places, the five-fold ministry gifts have been reduced to only two—pastoring and teaching. Those with the office mantles of evangelists, prophets, and apostles have been stoned and cast out of the vineyard. In the words of Christ, I can symbolically liken many of today's churches to Jerusalem in the gospels.

O Jerusalem, Jerusalem, thou that killest the prophets, and stonest them which are sent unto thee, how often would I have gathered thy children together, even as a hen gathereth her chickens under her wings, and ye would not! (Matt. 23:37; Luke 13:34).

Could this be the reason for the present collapse of many churches? Even in the western world, I see that the average age of church attenders is drastically increasing. [1]In the US, only 0.1 percent of church attendees in many Christian denominations are below thirty years of age, and the median age of across various churches is fifty-nine years. In contrast, Muslims and Hindus

118

in the US have a median age of thirty-three[6]! In England, the situation is a bit worse, as the average age of church attendees currently sits at sixty-one years[7].

The implication of all these analyses is clear. Any organization or movement without a vibrant youth group has no future. Except there is a divine intervention, the current trend in most churches calls for intentional prayers, strategic children and youth evangelism, and decisive discipleship of the next generation.

As I looked at several churches today, many of the younger generations are no longer in the church. Some have left due to leadership insensitivity to their plights and cries. Many have departed because of persecution from those who should have mentored them into fruition. Others have relapsed back into the world as water wells in many churches have run dry. There are pressing issues in the youths' world, but there seems to be no more water in the sanctuary to quench their thirst for answers. Many church leaders today are not equipped to help the lives of tomorrow's mighty men. In many assemblies, youths who remain in the church are just being used as numerical resources to submit reports. They have a form of godliness, but no experience of the power thereof. They know the Bible doctrines, but it has never become their personal experiences. Only very few youths have seen the days of divine encounters. The light seems to have gone out of the temple. The leadership appears to have gone to bed with the world.

Except for a scanty remnant, the manifestations of spiritual gifts have become scarce. For several years in many churches, there has been no fire, no tangible spiritual engagements, and no sustainable awakenings!

Second, I noticed that none of David's sons made it to the list of his mighty men. It bothers me to note that not even one could enter the list of *"workers or leaders"*! While there could be a good reason for this, I believe it might also be a bad thing to note in a leader's life. On a good note, it should be commendable if David did not put any of his kids on the list because they did not merit to be enlisted. However, on the other hand, it should be a concern to note if David was unable to train his kids to make this all-important list. Their noticeable absence tells a lot on the part of the king and his kids. Some Christian leaders have spent their entire life training other people's kids, but their kids are nowhere to be found in their ministry. What could have gone wrong? I am not writing this to blame or shame anyone. I am just raising an issue that I believe the Holy Spirit has whispered once and again in both the Old and New Testament scriptures.

> *Look not upon me, because I am black, because the sun hath looked upon me: my mother's children were angry with me; they made me the keeper of the vineyards; but mine own vineyard have I not kept* (S of S. 1:6).

> *But if any provide not for his own, and specially for those of his own house, he hath denied the faith, and is worse than an infidel* (1 Tim. 5:8).

If a leader of David's stature and strength did not do so well in this area, I believe this is an essential lesson for all living leaders and kingdom laborers to note. Children of Christian ministers must also recognize that anointing cannot be inherited. Everyone must meet the divine demands and pay the price for God's high calling to be relevant in life.

The third issue that I believe is paramount to God is managing human resources in the church. When the ministry was small, David managed his men well. However, it appeared that as his leadership strength increased, he seemed to begin to misuse his authority and power. Notably, David would not even cut his enemy's skirt before he became great. However, he killed anyone who disobeyed his orders or crossed his path after ascending the throne. Uriah disobeyed to his demise. Joab corrected or queried his omission to his disadvantage and eventual death sentence.

Fourth, it bothered me so much that David could waste the lives of precious men like Uriah and Joab without blinking an eye. Without fairness, he could discipline the same men who had jeopardized their lives to save his life and that of his family. David could fire the men God had used for him when his soul was in danger and turmoil. He punished the men he trained for putting to practice what he had taught them. Sadly, the situation has not changed much in our age. Why do churches and systems begin to persecute a person they once developed, the moment they start to manifest in glory? I believe it should be parents and mentors' prayers that their kids and mentees would go above and beyond them in achievements. I am afraid to confess that I have not seen many church leaders who sincerely wished for this. Did not Jesus allow His disciples to do greater things than He did while He was here on earth? Parents' glory is the success of their children, but it is sad to see many churches casting out their glory and future heritage. I have asked myself, why don't we celebrate our own? A church buries their future unwittingly when they criticize and persecute those they should be applauding and commemorating.

Jesus noted this during His earthly ministry, and He told us, "a prophet is not without honor, but in his own country, and among his own kindred, and in his own house" (Mark 6:4). By the time David was transitioning out of this world, his one-time undefeatable army had been politically polarized and scattered.

Fifth, you will agree that we live in the age of harvest. However, many of the faithful laborers are on the brink of retirement. They are tired but without a successor in view. I must say that God has been steadfast in sending laborers into His field. It is only unfortunate that the faithful laborers are not allowed to take their rightful places in the open fields of souls in many churches. Many times, when they are appointed, they are not allowed to do the bidding and wooing of heaven due to denominational sentiments and unfruitful traditions.

Sometimes, church leaders would not support ideas that would bring souls into the kingdom if it would not yield substantial financial returns. At other times, if you don't worship a church overseer as your "lord," they would see to it that they frustrate your journey. Such leaders have forgotten that the day of reckoning draws near. One cannot but wonder why the same set of leaders who claim to be praying for revival mistreat and persecute several faithful and honest disciples under them.

You are a leader, now or in the future! Church leadership is a good degree to be attained (1 Tim. 3:1, 13), but always remember that it is a privilege. It is a privilege to be the head, father, pastor, deacon, clergy, bishop, or overseer. None of us merits any position in the kingdom of God.

The sixth consideration is a counsel to every young and emerging leader. Let us be humble but honest. Make humility and holiness your priority. If you humble yourself, God will lift you up. The way up is down. Nevertheless, do not allow hypocrisy to creep into your life in an attempt to please men. If you do so, you will have disqualified yourself before God (Gal. 1:10). Men may lift you up because you know how to play along in church politics, but you must not mistake that to mean the approval of God. We must not be presumptuous, and we must not repeat the mistakes of Joab.

Finally, to everyone who has been leading in one capacity or the other, do not forget that you have only come this far by the grace of God (1 Cor. 15:10). Everyone is saved by grace—**from sin.**

*For by grace are ye saved through faith; and that **not of yourselves**: it is the gift of God: Not of works, **lest any man should boast** (Eph. 2:8).*

May the testimonies in this book never stand to witness against you at the end. After all your labors in this life, may your leadership position not become eternal regrets.

Many leaders are wallowing in hell now. Several people will still go from church offices, straight to hell (Matt. 7:22, 23). May God help you to walk circumspectly and act wisely.

ENDNOTES

1   National Sleep Foundation. Sleep problems & disorders: What are the facts about insomnia? https://www.sleep-foundation.org/articles/what-are-facts-about-insomnia. Assessed July 2020.

2   Penn Medicine News. 1 in 4 Americans Develop Insomnia Each Year. June 5, 2018. https://www.pennmedicine.org/news/news-releases/2018/june/1-in-4-americans-develop-insomnia-each-year. Assessed July 2020.

3   Thanksgiving day in Canada. https://www.timeanddate.com. Assessed July 2020.

4   John Wesley on giving. ResourceUMC. https://www.resourceumc.org/en/content/john-wesley-on-giving. Assessed July 2020

5   McCabe, Katie (August 1989). "Like Something the Lord Made." The Washingtonian. Retrieved 8 November 2014.

6   https://www.pewresearch.org/fact-tank/2016/07/11/which-u-s-religious-groups-are-oldest-and-youngest/ (Assessed August 2020).

7   Bloxham, Andy. "Average age of churchgoers now 61."
     The Telegraph. https://www.telegraph.co.uk/news/reli-
     gion/7054097/Average-age-of-churchgoers-now-61-
     Church-of-England-report-finds.html#:~:text=The%20
     average%20age%20of%20churchgoers,from%20the%20
     Church%20of%20England.&text=The%20report%2C%20
     compiled%20by%20the,in%20the%20pews%20are%20
     pensioners. (Accessed August 2020).

CPSIA information can be obtained
at www.ICGtesting.com
Printed in the USA
LVHW091327190221
679381LV00009B/776

9 781662 801600